D1295931

Decolonizing Feminisms

FEM

Laura E. Donaldson

decolonizing

NISMS

Race, Gender, & Empire-Building

The University of North Carolina Press   Chapel Hill & London

Manufactured in the
United States of America

96 95 94 93 92
5 4 3 2 1

Library of Congress
Cataloging-in-Publication Data
Donaldson, Laura E.
  Decolonizing feminisms : race, gender,
and empire-building / Laura E.
Donaldson.
      p. cm.
  Includes bibliographical references and
  index.
  ISBN 0-8078-2044-X (cloth : alk.
paper). — ISBN 0-8078-4382-2 (pbk. :
alk. paper)
    1. American literature—History and
criticism—Theory, etc.   2. English
literature—History and criticism—
Theory, etc.   3. Feminism and literature
—United States.   4. Feminism and
literature—Great Britain.
5. Imperialism in literature.   6. Colonies
in literature.   7. Sex role in literature.
8. Women in literature.   9. Race in
literature.   I. Title.
PS152.D58   1992
810.9′00082—dc20   92-54167
                    CIP

Chapter 1 originally appeared in
somewhat different form in *Diacritics* 18
(1988): 65–77.

Chapter 2 originally appeared in
somewhat different form in *Cinema
Journal* 29 (1990): 53–68 under the title,
"The King and I in Uncle Tom's Cabin,
or on the Borders of the Women's
Room."

Chapter 7 originally appeared in
somewhat different form in *Cultural
Critique* 11 (1988–89): 5–22.

Contents

Acknowledgments

I would like to thank the American Council of Learned Societies, whose research fellowship generously supported much of this project, and the Center for the Study of Women at the University of California, Los Angeles, where chapter 3 was conceived during a fall 1988 term as a Visiting Scholar. While numerous people contributed in both direct and indirect ways to this project, I would like to especially acknowledge the following: Giuseppe Mazzota, for his encouragement in entering the world of academic publishing; Leslie Rabine, for carefully reading chapters 1 and 7 and for being an inspiring "role model" even when she was not aware of it; Sandra Eisdorfer, for being a good friend as well as a superb editor; Elizabeth Meese and Susan Lanser, for extremely insightful, rigorous, and constructive readings of the whole text and for setting the standard in the conduct of feminist dialogue.

Finally, as usual in extended projects such as a book, families make an extraordinary contribution—emotionally, intellectually, and patiently. Mine is no different. Although it hardly seems adequate, I would like to express deepest gratitude to my husband, my parents, and those long-suffering four-legged saints, Hilda and Portia.

In short, the type of literary criticism suitable to the philosophy of praxis . . . must fuse the struggle for a new culture . . . and criticism of social life, feelings and conceptions of the world with aesthetic or purely artistic criticism, and it must do so with heat and passion.

Antonio Gramsci, "Problems of Criticism"

What Semiology must attack is not only, as in the days of My-thologies, the petit-bourgeois good conscience, but the symbolic and semantic system of our entire civilization; it is not enough to seek to change contents, we must above all aim at fissuring *the meaning-system itself: we must emerge from the Occidental enclosure.*

Roland Barthes, The Semiotic Challenge

Introduction

Scene 1: A workshop focusing on the problem of women and power in literature. One of the presenters (a white woman) persuasively details the emergence of a "postfeminist" consciousness in contemporary women's writing. A black woman on the panel challenges her analysis by arguing that such a characterization presupposes white feminism as the standard for *all* women's writing. For many African American women writers, she declares, feminism is only now blooming into full flower.

Scene 2: A conversation among an ethnically diverse group of colleagues in a university-based Women's Studies program. During this informal discussion, an African American woman announces to the group that "white women are not oppressed because they can marry white men."

Each of the scenes described above exhibits a misprision—a cultural and psychological misrecognition that I identify as the "Miranda Complex"—that threatens the continued viability of feminism as a revolutionary movement. Loosely taken from the interaction between Miranda and Caliban in Shakespeare's *The Tempest*, the Miranda Complex raises in a profoundly acute way the questions of sex and race and how feminists "read," or fail to read, their imbrication in theorizing women's lives. Scene 1 vividly illustrates how a predominantly white, middle-class feminism exhibits not an overt racism that conjures active dominance and enforced segregation but a more subtle "white solipsism" that passively colludes with a racist culture.[1] In too many instances, feminism has committed what revolutionary filmmaker Pier Paolo Pasolini describes (in his own gender-solipsistic language) as the greatest bourgeois offense—recuperating other life experiences by "not knowing how to recognize life experiences other than his own: and of bringing all other life experiences back to a substantial analogy with his own. It . . . performs an act that is the first step toward certain manifestations of the defense of his privileges and even toward racism. In this sense . . . there is no discontinuity between him and . . . an executioner in a concentration camp."[2] Pasolini's startling analogy between the brutal physical violence of an executioner and the epistemic violence of writing could also characterize the potential for violence within feminist criticism's denial of the diverse experiences and genders of the global community of women.

However, scene 2 is as monolithic in its own way as scene 1, since its heterosexism and lack of adequate class analysis lead the speaker to meld all white women together into undifferentiated economic and sexual categories and to ignore the social stratifications that divide white women from each other as well as from women of color. Such a homogenous stance also fails to perceive how women who enjoy the privileges accorded to middle-class whiteness can simultaneously experience sexual oppression. Marrying a white man with money does not necessarily mean freedom, since continued access to his economic and racial power depends upon a woman's acquiescence to a relationship that traditionally has inscribed her into the sexual hierarchies of patriarchy. In the final analysis, neither the participant in scene 1 nor in scene 2 acknowledges the complexity of women's material experience, and each exhibits a failure that stems from a too unitary and noncontradictory conception of gender.

Apropos of this shortcoming, the thread uniting the various essays and texts of this collection is my attempt to understand gender as a braid of complexly woven relationships and to formulate methods of feminist reading that are adequate to the task of analyzing its myriad strands. Further, if feminism affirms an inseparable connection between theory and praxis, then the notion of gender as a heterogenous ensemble calls for a similar heterogeneity of critical methods in analyzing its mobile and tensive relationships. Just as the title to this book pluralizes "feminism," I pluralize "method" in the preceding sentence because, as Donna Przybylowicz notes in her essay "Toward a Feminist Cultural Criticism: Hegemony and Modes of Social Division":

A particularly fruitful and oppositional feminist cultural theory would be one that uses various methodologies but that also takes a symptomatic stance towards its own discourse. Employing poststructuralist, psychoanalytic, and contemporary Marxist analyses in order to study, contest, and dismantle patriarchal structures, it does not internalize and identify with nor uncritically and exclusively use these approaches. Rather, in critiquing as well as engaging with them in the process of transforming the asymmetrical forms of power based on gender/race/class exploitation, it perceives meaning as contradictory and dialectical and society as the product of a divisive and dialogical process.[3]

This work emulates such a process by drawing upon a number of different reading strategies, including deconstruction, Marxism, and feminist film criticism. Although my choice of strategies reflects my own position, both in the academy and in the "divisive and dialogical" dynamics of society, it also favors those strategies that highlight the intricately carved surfaces of women's experience. Indeed, *Decolonizing Feminisms* attempts to counter feminism's imperialist tendency to dive deep and surface with a single hermeneutic truth by articulating reading practices that privilege horizontal relationships, not only within women's narrative texts but also gender identities themselves.

Chapter 1 thematizes what Chandra Talpade Mohanty calls white feminism's "discursive" colonization of the "Third World" woman in the critical exchange over the figure of Bertha Mason—the woman from the colonies. This chapter explores how, on the one hand, Sandra Gilbert and Susan Gubar's enormously influential *Madwoman in the Attic: The Woman Writer and the Nineteenth-Century Imagination* contributes to a white solipsistic reading of "women's material and historical heterogeneities by producing/re-presenting the madwoman in *Jane Eyre*'s attic as a composite, singular . . . image which appears arbitrarily constructed, but nevertheless carries with it the authorizing signature of Western humanist discourse."[4] On the other hand, Gayatri Chakravorty Spivak's essay, "Three Women's Texts and a Critique of Imperialism," corrects Gilbert and Gubar by assigning to Jane an individualist and imperialist Anglo-European masculinity that distorts the novel's ideological construction of her identity. I offer an alternative reading of *Jane Eyre* that attempts to move feminist criticism beyond the political conundrums posed by each of these ultimately problematic positions.

However one defines the specifics of discursive and historical colonialism, they both imply a relation of structural domination and an often violent suppression of the heterogeneity of the colonized subject.[5] Chapters 2 through 4 address this process by "proceeding along coincidental axes of identities with a problematic capacity to identify anything in particular, simultaneous and irreducible differentials, not just of sex, but of race, class, and sexual orientation."[6] For example, chapter 2, "The King and I in Uncle Tom's Cabin; or, On the Borders of the Women's Room: Race, Gender, and Sexual Difference," and chapter 3, "The Con of the Text: Textualism, Contextualism, and Anticolonialist Feminist Theories," read the historical memoirs of Anglo-European women through their contemporary mediations in film. Each of these memoirs, Anna Leonowens's *The English Governess at the Siamese Court: Being Recollections of Six Years in the Royal Palace at Bangkok* and Mrs. Aeneas Gunn's *We of the Never-Never* and *The Little Black Princess*, are embedded within the historical context of imperialist England in the nineteenth and early twentieth centuries, and each has been appropriated for a postmodern generation in successful and critically acclaimed films (*The King and I* and *We of the Never-Never*, respectively). Reading women's historical experience in the interstices between autobiographical inscription and filmic representation allows one to explore gender as a variable between different forms of discourse[7]—here, between the discourses of Anglo-European colonialism and Western patriarchal representation.

Chapter 2 foregrounds the question of gender identity by grappling with it as a variable between the contradictory discourses of human rights, True Womanhood, abolitionism, and colonialism that construct the figure of "Mrs. Anna" in her memoirs and in *The King and I*. Chapter 3 complements chapter 2's analysis of gender identity through its attempt to extend the feminist tradition of ideological reading by developing a postcolonial and poststruc-

turalist trope: graf(ph)ting. Both chapters dramatize how historical colonialism forces an intervention in feminist social and literary criticism and fractures any univocal reading, either of women's
experience or of women's texts.

Ironically, an exploration of women's actual historical experience within colonialism and our own era's representation of that
experience problematizes the man=colonizer, woman=colonized
metaphor that feminism has often used to analyze women's oppression. For example, in *Women, Resistance, and Revolution: A
History of Women and Revolution in the Modern World*, Sheila
Rowbotham perceives that "certain similarities exist between the
colonization of the underdeveloped country and female oppression
within capitalism. There is the economic dependence, the cultural
take-over, the identification of dignity with resemblance to the
oppressor."[8] Contemporary feminism has not only continued but
expanded this metaphor. Josephine Donovan notes in her essay
"Towards a Women's Poetics" that "women, whether in community or isolation, share a condition of oppression, or otherness,
that is imposed by governing patriarchal or androcentric ideologies. Women as a group, therefore, share certain awarenesses that
are common to oppressed groups."[9]

Marilyn French's *Beyond Power: On Men, Women, and Morals*
offers one of the most extended elaborations of the man=colo-
nizer, woman=colonized homology in its claim that "if we trans-
pose the descriptions of colonized and colonizer to women and
men, they fit at almost every point."[10] Like the relationship of
colonizer to colonized, Western culture has defined women as different in kind from men and has often used animal imagery to
dramatize this difference. Just as colonizers deny colonized persons their right to own property and a share in the economic means
of production, men have denied this same right to women: "Like
slavemasters and colonizers they have expected women to identify
their interests with their oppressors'" (*BP* 131). Finally, according
to French, just as colonization denies the colonized a voice in their
own culture, most women in most cultures "have not been deprived just of a cultural voice, but even a personal one" (*BP* 134).
This image possesses undeniable power in articulating the oppres-

sion of many women; yet, it is also symptomatic of what Homi K. Bhabha calls an imperialist cross-referencing that denies the metonymy of the colonial moment.[11] Recuperating the experience of the "Other" as a signifier of women's experience, it actually functions as a "narrative ruse" whose search for "cultural commensurability" ethnocentrically elides the colonized's ambivalent, hybrid knowledges.[12]

Further, the woman=colonized, man=colonizer metaphor lacks any awareness of gender—or colonialism, for that matter—as a contested field, an overdetermined sociopolitical grid whose identity points are often contradictory. Historical colonialism demonstrates the political as well as theoretical necessity of abandoning the idea of women's (and men's) gender identity as fixed and coherent. Instead, it imbues us with a conception of gender as a site of conflicting subjective processes and makes it impossible to ignore the contradictory social positioning of white, middle-class women as both colonized patriarchal objects and colonizing race-privileged subjects. However, it is precisely this contradiction that classical Marxism, one of the most powerful accounts of both colonialism and human identity, ignores.

In *Women's Oppression Today: Problems in Marxist Feminist Analysis*, Michèle Barrett remarks that the determinist model of classical Marxism is extremely weak when it theorizes subjectivity in other than the most simple class terms.[13] For example, the classical Marxist explanation of subjectivity in terms of economic modes of production would have great difficulty interpreting Albert Memmi's moving description of a heterogenous subjectivity forged in the throes of North African colonialism: "My portrait of the colonized, which is very much my own, is preceded by a portrait of the colonizer. How could I have permitted myself, with all my concern about personal experience, to draw a portrait of the adversary? Here is a confession I have never made before: I know the colonizer from the inside almost as well as I know the colonized."[14] Part of the reason for Marxism's difficulty with Memmi's confession is its failure to account for the profound imbrication within the human subject of multiple, and often contesting, discourses. For Memmi, these would include the discourses of French colonialism that interpellate Tunisians as the colonized Other and the anti-Muslim discourses of European Judaism and Christianity that bestow upon Memmi's Jewishness a privileged status.

Chapter 4, based on another reading of *We of the Never-Never*, addresses this weakness in classical Marxism by examining the colonialist discourse of the "piccaninny" and interrogating how discourses of race and sex become threaded through each other in order to foster the goals of white supremacy and patriarchy. During the course of this interrogation, chapter 4 suggests ways for re-visioning Marxism's stance toward "the gender-saturated" nature of all social relations.[15] The discourse of the "piccaninny" also dramatizes the necessity of any feminist cultural theory to attend to the "Marxist linking of ideology with material interests and its integral role in the reproduction of specific forms of power relations in society."[16] As we have seen, many feminist discussions overlook the material specificity of gender and assign women's place within gender ideology according to the machinations of an ahistorical patriarchy. If Marxism ignores the gender-saturated nature of all class relations, then feminism often ignores the racially saturated nature of all gender relations. The reading strategies elaborated in chapter 4 put each of these standpoints into a creative and, hopefully, productive tension with one another.

Feminist film critics have noted that Western visual representation usually perpetuates a man=subject, woman=object dichotomy. Chapter 5, "A Passage to 'India': Colonialism and Filmic Representation," demonstrates how David Lean's highly acclaimed and popular 1984 filmic adaptation of E. M. Forster's novel extends this dichotomy by requiring viewers to become armchair colonialists who are unwittingly sutured into the gaze of the colonizer. Like *The King and I*, the content of Lean's film seems to subvert the equation of colonized=object, colonizer=subject; yet, also like *The King and I*, its own signifying practices place the content in contradiction. Chapter 5 shows not only the continuing power of colonialism to deform any liberatory politics but also the difficulty of excavating a genuinely postcolonial space for feminism. In this context, chapter 5 widens the argument for postcolonial subjectivities and reading practices that affirm the interweaving of oppressions rather than their hierarchical privileging.

Although my discussion of *A Passage to India* deals primarily with Western culture's reading of gender, race, and empire-building, one should also note how the texts of both Forster and Lean simultaneously focus the question of homosocial desire as well. "Homosocial," according to Eve Kosofsky Sedgwick, is a neologism that is just as obviously formed by its analogy with the term "homosexual" as it is meant to be distinguished from this term: "In fact, it is applied to such activities as 'male bonding,' which may, as in our society, be characterized by intense homophobia, fear and hatred of homosexuality." [17] The extremely insulated triangular relationship between Mr. Turton (the tax collector), Major Callendar, and Ronny Heaslop (magnificently summarized in Mr. Turton's statement that "Heaslop's a sahib; he's the type we want, he's one of us") construes "India" as a field traversed by the structures of homosocial desire. Or, in the words of Sedgwick, "Kim's India is . . . a kind of postgraduate or remedial Public School, a male place in which it is relatively safe for men to explore the crucial terrain of homosociality." [18] I emphasize this point because homosocial desire acts as a kind of textual unconscious for the entire discussion of empire.

Nationalism has historically functioned as one of the most powerful weapons for resisting colonialism and for establishing the space of a postcolonial identity. One reason nationalism assumes such an important role in this century stems from the fact that, in much of the contemporary world, the concept of "nation" resolves questions of identity by signifying that larger reality to which particular social groups belong.[19] As Cornelius Castoriadis notes in *The Imaginary Institution of Society*, the nation has become "this 'us,'" which is "first of all, a symbol, the insignias of existence that every tribe, every city, every society has always ascribed to itself." [20] Nationalism has also nurtured much of the movement toward women's emancipation in Asia, Africa, and South America. Kumari Jayawardena, in her introduction to *Feminism and Nationalism in the Third World*, observes that

"Third World" feminism "was acted out against a background of nationalist struggles aimed at achieving political independence, asserting a national identity, and modernizing society."[21]

For our purposes, the most important of these three aims is the assertion of a national identity, which Jayawardena acknowledges as the linchpin in mobilizing peoples, and especially women, against imperialism. Yet feminism and nationalism have developed an uneasy, if not antagonistic, relationship because of the often conflicting nature of their social and political goals. On the one hand, feminism has attempted to empower a community of women that transcends cultural characteristics and geographic boundaries; on the other hand, nationalism has exaggerated such characteristics and boundaries in order to resist hegemonic occupation. Frantz Fanon has criticized positions such as feminism's for their "neo-liberal universalism," while Rosa Luxemburg, in her famous debate with Lenin, opposed nationalism for fostering parochialism and fragmenting international revolutionary movements. Both of these criticisms have some validity. Much of *Decolonizing Feminisms* devotes itself to analyzing the ways in which feminism's universalist stance disguises its white, middle-class solipsism and recuperates the experience of diverse groups of women. Further, if—as I would assert—liberating strategies must arise from the concrete historical circumstances of each oppressed group, then one cannot dismiss any strategies per se without some concrete knowledge of each particular situation.

However, even the most benevolent manifestations of nationalism are limited in their potential for effecting change. As Julius Nyerere, president of Tanzania and theorist of the new African nationalism, observes: "The task of the nationalist is simply to rouse the people to a confidence in their own power of protest. But to build the real freedom which socialism represents is a very different thing. It demands a positive understanding and positive actions, not simply a rejection of colonialism and a willingness to cooperate in noncooperation."[22] In its more malevolent manifestations—such as seen throughout Europe during the two world wars—nationalism transforms confidence into demagoguery and rejection into legitimation of violence. This lethal cultivation of national identity during the world wars is the background for chapter 6, "Rereading Moses/Rewriting Exodus: The Postcolonial Imagination of Zora Neale Hurston." This chapter focuses on a potentially liberating nexus between deconstruction and the politics of identity through Zora Neale Hurston's rewriting of the Exodus story in her novel, *Moses, Man of the Mountain* (1939).

Hurston's novel along with Virginia Woolf's *Three Guineas* (1938)[23] provide two of the most profound critiques of nationalism extant in the modern world. Both women wrote "with the sound of the guns in [their] ears" (*TG* 4) and both women lived on the margins of their respective societies: Woolf as bisexual and female in the heterosexual, masculinist society of England, and Hurston as black and female in the whitemale supremacist society of America. Both Woolf and Hurston were haunted by the specter of Hitler's "beast" devouring Europe. Indeed, in one of *Three Guineas*'s most powerfully prophetic passages, Woolf draws a parallel between sexism and racism (an analogy whose parallelism does not depend on imperialist cross-referencing), which oppress by maintaining the "difference" of women and nonwhites, and nationalism, which often fanatically promulgates the "difference" between cultures:

> And abroad the monster has come more openly to the surface. There is no mistaking him there. He has widened his scope. He is interfering now with your liberty; he is dictating how you shall live; he is making distinctions not merely between the sexes, but between the races. You are feeling in your own person what your mothers felt when they were shut out, when they were shut up, because they were women. Now you are being shut out, you are being shut up, because you are Jews, because you are democrats, because of race, because of religion. . . . The whole iniquity of dictatorship, whether in Oxford or Cambridge, in Whitehall or Downing Street, against Jews or against women, in England or in Germany, in Italy or in Spain is now apparent to you. (*TG* 102–3)

"Making distinctions": not just devaluing but, in the case of Hitler, annihilating difference. It is this logic of opposition— this uncritical construction of an exclusive Self and an excluded

Other—which links sexism, racism, and nationalism and brings nationalism as a postcolonial feminist strategy deeply into question.

Barely a year after Woolf published *Three Guineas*, Zora Neale Hurston boldly strode into the global theater with a work every bit as controversial and profound in its critique of nationalism and ethnocentrism. *Moses, Man of the Mountain* establishes Hurston as a woman without a country, along with Woolf: "As a woman, I have no country. As a woman I want no country. As a woman my country is the whole world" (*TG* 109). Indeed, it is this text and its deconstructive rewriting of the Exodus that form *Decolonizing Feminisms*'s transition from colonialism to postcolonialism and usher us—literally and semantically—into the final chapter, "(ex)Changing (wo)Man: Toward a Materialist-Feminist Semiotics."

The interior chapters of the book are framed by two methodological attempts to discover more adequate bases for feminist readings: chapter 1, which critiques a hermeneutics of suspicion complicit with the agendas of imperialism, and chapter 7, which suggests a more heterogenous model through its articulation of gender identity as "allegorical." While chapter 7 is not as explicitly concerned with historical colonialism as the other chapters, its importance lies in the methodological contribution it makes to the development of a postcolonial feminism, which draws upon the social critiques of such materialist discourses as Marxism and the critique of identity contained in poststructuralism. Although I address this issue more fully in the Postscript, it seems important to note that one effect of forging feminism from such univocal terms as "sexual difference" and "sisterhood" is the reduction of the Other to the same—an impulse at the heart of the colonialist project.

Through the twists and turns of *Decolonizing Feminisms*, I hope to empower the postcolonial reader who, in the words of Gayatri Chakravorty Spivak, adopts "the careful project of unlearning our privilege as our loss."[24] As Spivak notes in an interview with Elizabeth Grosz, this unlearning will not come through benevolence or good intentions; rather, its voyage must be meticulously plotted, point by agonizing point, and then strategically used to make visible the previously invisible ways that power has penetrated women's experience. The particular coordinates of this book represent my own historical preoccupations and chart some particular social and theoretical concerns. The remainder of feminism's postcolonial journey awaits other navigators, other ships, and other trajectories. May they safely reach their destinations.

Colonialism and the Question
of Feminist Reading

1

—

The Miranda Complex

Mir.: The strangeness of your story put heaviness in me.
Pros.: Shake it off. Come on. We'll visit Caliban, my slave, who
    never yields us kind answer.
Mir.: 'Tis a villain, sir, I do not love to look on.
               The Tempest, 1.2.372–78

Blindness slashes our tapestry to shreds.
Audre Lorde, Our Dead behind Us: Poems

In the novel *Invisible Man*—Ralph Ellison's profound exploration of a black man's invisibility within a white man's world—seeing (or not seeing) is the paradigmatic political and hermeneutic act. This is particularly true in an episode that focuses upon the importance of race as an interpretive framework for the Brotherhood, the leftist group that has recruited the Invisible Man as a paid organizer. After the police arrest an unarmed black man for selling Little Black Sambo dolls without a permit and then shoot him for resisting arrest, a heated argument erupts between the Invisible Man and Brother Tobitt, a leader of the leftist group. Tobitt emphatically rejects the contention that race had anything to do with this killing: "Black and white, white and black . . . must we listen to this racist nonsense?"[1] The Invisible Man retorts that he was only trying "to point out a part of reality which the committee seems to have missed" (*IM* 461).

This blindness of the Brotherhood is ironically dramatized when, during a fit of rage, Brother Tobitt's glass eye pops out. Tobitt's dead "buttermilk" eye becomes a powerful emblem of how those who *should* see cannot perceive difference and of how this incarcerates the Invisible Man in a social and political transparency: "I am invisible, understand, simply because people refuse to see me. . . . When they approach me they see only my surroundings, themselves, or figments of their imagination—indeed, everything and anything except me. Nor is my invisibility exactly a matter of a biochemical accident to my epidermis. That invisibility to which I refer occurs because of a peculiar disposition of the eyes of those with whom I come into contact. A matter of the construction of their *inner* eyes, those eyes with which they look through their physical eyes upon reality" (*IM* 3). The true failure, then, is that of the inner eye—the hermeneutic eye—which selects some random elements of reality and foregrounds them as meaningful patterns but relegates others to a meaningless background. If, as the Invisible Man suggests, responsibility rests on recognition and recognition is a form of agreement, then the Brotherhood belies its name in the "peculiar disposition" of its eyes and its coercive erasure of the Other.

It is precisely this agreement about recognition that is lacking in the recent tempests of feminist literary theory. Instead of the Invisible Man, however, there looms the Invisible Woman—the character of Bertha Mason in Charlotte Brontë's novel, *Jane Eyre*. In fact, one of this decade's most influential works of critical theory, Sandra Gilbert and Susan Gubar's *The Madwoman in the Attic: The Woman Writer and the Nineteenth-Century Imagination*, takes its name from Bertha—the madwoman hidden and confined in the attic of Thornfield—and uses her as the pivotal figure in re-visioning an alternative literary tradition manifesting "the common, female impulse to struggle free from social and literary confinement through strategic redefinitions of self, art and society."[2]

For Gilbert and Gubar, Bertha expresses the "anxieties and abilities" of this feminine tradition: as Jane's "truest and darkest double she is the . . . ferocious secret self Jane has been trying to repress ever since her days at Gateshead" (*MA* 360). Indeed, they argue, only Jane's absorption of Bertha's character into her own allows her to achieve the fully sexual and independent identity that she lacks throughout most of Brontë's text. However, in her essay "Three Women's Texts and a Critique of Imperialism," Gayatri Chakravorty Spivak criticizes the adoption of *Jane Eyre* as a limit text of feminism since it privileges the individualist female subject who, "not-quite/not-male," articulates herself in such a way that the " 'native female' . . . (within discourse, as a signifier) is excluded from any share in this emerging norm."[3] For Spivak, the articulation of feminist identity all too often repeats what she characterizes as the quintessential gesture of colonialism—blindness to the epistemic violence that effaces the colonial subject and requires her to occupy the space of the imperialists' self-consolidating Other.[4]

This position of the self-consolidating Other clearly describes the space that Bertha occupies in Gilbert and Gubar's interpretation of *Jane Eyre*. As Rochester's first wife, Bertha is the obstacle preventing his and Jane's ultimate happiness; as the white Jamaican Creole who "grovelled, seemingly, on all fours . . . and growled like some strange wild animal," she blurs the frontier between human and animal and justifies the project of "soul making" that Spivak identifies with the imperialist project; finally, as a representative of the creolized, or "mixed," scene of Europe and its "not-yet-human Other" (*TWT* 247), Bertha sacrifices her own identity so that Jane might find hers. Spivak's questioning of *Jane Eyre* as a limit text of feminism implies that Bertha functions as its rem(a)inder of slavery, for she reminds us of the theoretical diaspora in which the "native" female subject is remaindered—sold out, discontinued, dropped.

This criticism seems particularly telling in view of Gilbert and Gubar's interpretation of Bertha in *Madwoman*, which deprives her of any independent textual significance by confining her to the privatistic cell of Jane's psyche. Further, their placement of Bertha within that genre of women's fantasies "in which maddened doubles functioned as asocial surrogates for docile selves" (*MA* xi) irrevocably alienates her from both history and culture. Indeed, Gilbert and Gubar's regret concerning "just how much . . . women's history has been lost or misunderstood" (*MA* xii) ironically underscores the limitations of their own position, since their own "distinctively female" tapestry bleaches women of color into an asocial invisibility. Like the Invisible Man, women of color learn that "I may not-see myself as others see me not" (*IM* 466).

A construct that might help us understand the discursive colonialism implied by this extraordinarily difficult and paradigmatic situation within feminism is taken from Shakespeare's play *The Tempest* and illustrated by what I call the "Miranda Complex." While the trope of Prospero and Caliban and its evocation of self and other, the West and the Rest of Us, the colonizer and the indigenous people, has received much critical attention,[5] the relationship between Miranda and Caliban has been virtually ignored. In the symbolic economy of the "Prospero Complex," Prospero enacts the role of omnipotent Western patriarch, and Caliban, that of the "native" Other suffering from the cultural deracination which serves as the intellectual and emotional counterpart to economic enslavement.[6] However, Miranda—the Anglo-European daughter—offers us a feminine "spin" on this complex, for her textual selflessness in *The Tempest* produces the character effect of women's oppression under the rule of their biological and cultural Fathers. One could argue that, like Caliban, Miranda has been "colonized and tricked" and exists only "as man's other side, his denied, abused, and hidden side. She has constantly been the embodiment of a nonculture."[7] A crucial question raised by the coupling of Miranda with Caliban, then, is why these two victims of colonialist Prosperity cannot "see" each other, and it is here that the analogies posited within either complex begin to decompose and destabilize any attempt to imbue them with noncontradictory meanings.

Most interpreters of the Prospero Complex have construed Caliban solely in terms of his status as a displaced colonized object, but few have perceived Caliban's own quest for mastery through one of the patriarchal theater's most "disastrous rehearsals of enforced heterosexuality"[8]—attempted rape. Caliban sees in Miranda only the distorted being of a woman whose possession not only would visit poetic justice upon the colonizer but also grant vicarious patronymic power. As Jeffner Allen observes in *Lesbian Philosophy: Explorations*, men use rape as a weapon of revenge against other men and as an infringement on other men's property (*LP* 40); rape becomes in effect "a monologue by men about an invisible woman" (*LP* 41). Caliban's overdetermined participation in imperialism and masculinism as both victim and victimizer radically questions any construction of him as the homogenous colonized Other of the Prospero Complex. It does, however, account for his unstable signification within the Miranda Complex, for his erasure of Miranda as the invisible woman prevents him from grasping how similarly Prospero dominates both "daughter" and "native." Trapped in this vicious paradox, Caliban reinforces, rather than weakens, the chains of their mutual enslavement.

Given this threat of rape, it is not hard to discern why Miranda describes the son of Sycorax as a "villain" that she does "not love to look on." Yet, the peculiarities of Miranda's own position emerge in her status as the sexual object of both the Anglo-European male and the native Other and as the loyal daughter/wife who ultimately aligns herself with the benefits and protection offered by the colonizing father and husband. Thus, the Miranda Complex does not allow us to create the easy identification of Miranda with white feminist literary criticism or of Caliban with the woman from the colonies. Both positions are too traversed by contradiction to sustain any such univocal homologies. Rather, the Prospero and Miranda complexes should become parables about the dangers of monotheistic reading, that is, reading structured so tightly by a single principle (whether emanating either from the West or the Rest of Us) that it excludes all other interpretive categories. If the tempest is a havoc raised by mastery (or complicity in mastery),[9] it spawns uncomfortable ideological questions about the enabling conditions of feminist reading.

"That's French," Harker told me then, and dropped down beside me
where I was sitting there on the ground. . . . "Negro" meant black
man; "negress" was black woman; "blank" was white. I laughed at
that, thinking about Miz Lady.

Sherley Anne Williams, *Dessa Rose*

White mythology—metaphysics has erased within itself the fabulous scene that has produced it, the scene that nevertheless remains
active and stirring, inscribed in white ink, an invisible design covered
over in the palimpsest.

Jacques Derrida, "White Mythology"

In their interpretation of a distinctively female literary tradition,
Gilbert and Gubar follow the example of Marx and Freud by constructing a "hermeneutics of suspicion," or the search for a deep
truth buried beneath layer upon layer of social and cultural sedi-
ment. For Marx, the fetishism of the commodity hides the scene
of its social production; for Freud, the repressive forces of the
conscious hide the sexual scene of the unconscious; for Gilbert
and Gubar, the masculinist literary tradition hides the feminine
"truth" of the woman's text-palimpsest: "In short . . . women from
Jane Austen and Mary Shelley to Emily Brontë and Emily Dickin-
son produced literary works that are in some sense palimpsestic,
works whose surface designs conceal or obscure deeper, less ac-
cessible (and less socially acceptable) levels of meaning. Thus these
authors managed the difficult task of achieving true female literary
authority by simultaneously conforming to and subverting patriarchal literary standards" (*MA* 73). In the woman's text-palimpsest,
a surface design created by the conventions of "male genre" covers
over an invisible, and often subversive, inscription of an alternative
"female" sensibility. Reading consequently becomes an activity
of salvaging the authentic, yet submerged, female literary voice.
Gilbert and Gubar's more general description of feminist methodology clearly supports this characterization of their work as a
hermeneutics of suspicion: "Because so many of the lost or concealed truths of female culture have recently been retrieved by

feminist scholars, women readers in particular have lately become aware that nineteenth-century literary women felt they had things to hide" (*MA* 75). However, unlike Marx or Freud, who posit a negative motivation for the social or sexual repression of the truth, Gilbert and Gubar assert a positive one: hiding the female voice enables it to survive the crushing weight of an overtly hostile literary tradition.

Of course then the question becomes what exactly *is* the "single secret message" (*MA* 75) of their feminist hermeneutics? Gilbert and Gubar resoundingly affirm that it does possess a univocal content and its name is Bertha Mason: her "figure arises like a bad dream, bloody, envious, enraged, as if the very process of writing had itself liberated a madwoman, a crazy and angry woman, from a silence in which neither she nor her author can continue to acquiesce" (*MA* 77). The blindness induced by this monotheistic reading of Bertha as the white feminist's nightmare seemingly confirms Spivak's claim that feminist methodology requires "a self-immolating colonial subject for the glorification of the social mission of the colonizer" (TWT 251)—or the annihilation of the "native" female Bertha for the glory of Jane's individuation. While the most obvious element of this determining pattern is the way Bertha's "mad" voice screams with the anger of all women, a less obvious element emerges in the privilege that Gilbert and Gubar bestow upon the first terms in the binary oppositions depth-surface and invisible-visible in their re-creation of the woman's text-palimpsest—a hierarchy that prevents them from perceiving how nonwhite mythologies might offer a very different model of reading.

This "Other" politics of reading resists Gilbert and Gubar's attempt to locate an invisible truth beneath the visible surface of the text's signifying practices by demanding that we interrogate *figures* of the feminine Other in all their phenomenal immediacy. For example, the interpretive act within the black literary tradition turns on the signifying trope of Eshu, the trickster-linguist figure of Yoruban mythology.[10] Eshu's feminine counterpart exists in Pomba Gira, his cunning and voluptuous Brazilian wife, who cultivates ambiguity by showing one palm upward, as if bestowing favor, and the other downward, as if denying it.[11] As an interpretive model from a non-European culture, Pomba Gira figures an undecidability that requires the reader of a text—in this case, of a woman's facial expression—to engage in traversing its surface rather than diving deep and surfacing (to use a well-known feminist metaphor) with the sunken hermeneutic treasure.

Zora Neale Hurston's ethnography of hoodoo, "or Voodoo as pronounced by the whites," [12] dramatizes how a strategy of reading that does not privilege binary opposition might operate. According to Hurston, hoodoo thrived in the black communities of the South as a religion of the oppressed whose rituals particularly endowed women with its power of reading signs. All hoodoo practitioners must become adept at reading signs, for they must know the meaning of phenomena that occur in nature, the weather, the behavior of plant and animal life, and the whims of children. To the hoodoo sign-reader, all these have spiritual significance. [13]

Hurston brings this process of reading to life in her description of the conjurer Frizzly Rooster and how he "worked" his clients: "He could 'read' anybody at sight. He could 'read' anyone who remained out of his sight if they but stuck two fingers inside the door. He could 'read' anyone, no matter how far away, if he were given their height and color." [14] Unlike Gilbert and Gubar, then, the hoodoo sign-reader conjures a heterogenous rather than homogenous signifying practice, for the reader of the hoodoo text, "like all of the conjure masters, has more than one way of doing every job. People are different and what will win with one person has no effect upon another." [15] As an-Other strategy of reading, hoodoo demands that one attend to the surface of the text and refuse to subsume its plurivocity into the quest for an underlying feminine truth.

A WOMANIST READING OF *JANE EYRE*

Womanist 1. From "womanish" (Opp. of "girlish," i.e., frivolous, irresponsible, not serious). A black feminist or feminist of color. From the black folk expression of mothers to female children, "You acting womanish, i.e., like a woman. Usually referring to outrageous, audacious, courageous or *willfull* behavior. Wanting to know more and in greater depth than is considered "good" for one. . . . 2. *Also*:

Traditionally capable, as in: "Mama, I'm walking to Canada and
I'm taking you and a bunch of other slaves with me." Reply: "It
wouldn't be the first time."

Alice Walker, *In Search of Our Mothers' Gardens*

Frantz Fanon observed in *Black Skin, White Masks* that "the only
means of breaking this vicious circle that throws me back on myself is to restore to the other, through mediation and recognition,
his human reality. . . . The other has to perform the same operation. 'Action from one side only would be useless, because what
is to happen can only be brought about by means of both.'"[16]
Fanon's statement foregrounds the weakness in the position not
only of Gilbert and Gubar but also of Spivak in "Three Women's
Texts." Spivak's failure to see how the white woman, as well as
the "native" subject, suffers the ravages of colonialism not only
calls her problematic of "feminist individualism in the age of imperialism" into question but also raises grave questions about any
politics of reading that privileges one oppression over another.
Barbara Smith drives this point "home" in *Home Girls: A Black
Feminist Anthology* when she declares that "we [women of color]
examined our lives and found that everything out there was kicking
our behinds—race, class, sex, and homophobia. We saw no reason
to rank oppressions, or, as many forces in the Black community
would have us do, to pretend that sexism, among all the isms, was
not happening to us."[17] This description of "womanism" affirms
the interweaving of oppressions and incorporates sexual, racial,
cultural, national, and economic considerations into any politics
of reading.[18]

If the critical practice of *Madwoman* precludes a womanist ethic
by its domestication and dissimulation of the "native" Other, then
the practice of "Three Women's Texts" seems equally problematic
in its presupposition that *Jane Eyre* perpetuates the individualist subject through the subjectivity of Jane herself (TWT 224).
According to Louis Althusser in "Ideology and Ideological State
Apparatuses," the classic realist text interpellates or constructs the
relationship between narrative and reader so that the reading subject willingly accepts her status as the individual and noncontradictory locus of meaning. Spivak uses Althusser's formulation to

argue that Jane's "privatization" in the opening of Brontë's text (exemplified by Jane's withdrawal from the dining room peopled by the Reed family into a subsidiary and isolated breakfast room) implies a "self-marginalized uniqueness" fertile with the ideology of bourgeois individualism. In Spivak's analysis, *Jane Eyre* as a feminist tract bears the offspring "militant female subject" (TWT 244–45), a woman who achieves her identity at the expense of the "native," not quite human, female Other.

This conclusion points to a weakness within Althusser's theory: because interpellation ignores the fissures that the violent and subterranean pressures of patriarchal society open between men and women, its uncritical adoption can lead one into false assumptions. Indeed, a false conflation of masculine and feminine subject positions certainly underlies Spivak's statement that "Gilbert and Gubar, by calling *Jane Eyre* 'Plain Jane's progress,' see the novel as simply replacing the male protagonist [of *Pilgrim's Progress*] with the female" (TWT 249). For Gilbert and Gubar, however, *Jane Eyre* parodies, rather than reproduces, the structure of the masculine quest plot and consequently narrates a distinctively feminine story of enclosure and escape (*MA* 314).

By contending that Jane's establishment of spatial and psychological boundaries connotes an "individualist" differentiation and autonomy, Spivak endows Jane with qualities usually ascribed to masculine development within the capitalist patriarchal family. Nancy Chodorow notes in *The Reproduction of Mothering: Psychoanalysis and the Sociology of Gender* that the separation of the postoedipal boy from the mother requires him to engage in a more emphatic individuation and a more defensive firming of experienced ego boundaries than the postoedipal girl.[19] However, Jane's internalized practices of oppression—a "habitual mood of humiliation, self-doubt, forlorn depression"—place her in a subject(ed) position starkly contrasted to the masculine one iterated by Chodorow and assigned to her by Spivak. As her last name suggests, Jane is invisible as air and the heir to nothing (*MA* 342).

However, if we traverse the textual surface of *Jane Eyre*, a surface whose filmic qualities are much more pronounced than is usually realized, another interpretation of the relationship between Jane and Bertha emerges. Through the processes of cinematic suture, we glimpse a critical strategy more promising than Althusserian interpellation—not only for reading Brontë's very complex woman's text but also for developing a womanist politics of reading. Unlike interpellation, suture articulates itself in relation to culturally imposed differences between the positions of men and women: "As a process, a practice of signification, suture is an ideological operation with a particular function in relation to paternal ideology in that out of a system of differences it establishes a position in relation to the phallus. In so doing it places the spectator in relation to that position. . . . It is the imaginary unity, the sutured coherence, the imaginary sense of identity set up by the classic film which must be challenged by a feminist film practice to achieve a different constitution of the subject in relation to ideology."[20] If we imagine that Jane's "I" has become the "eye" of a camera, Spivak's characterization of her as a whitemale individualist Self becomes much more questionable:

I now stood in the empty hall; before me was the breakfast-room door, and I stopped, intimidated and trembling. What a miserable little poltroon had fear, engendered of unjust punishment, made of me in those days! I feared to return to the nursery, and feared to go forward to the parlour; ten minutes I stood in agitated hesitation; the vehement ringing of the breakfast-room bell decided me; I *must* enter.

"Who could want me?" I asked inwardly, as with both hands I turned the stiff door-handle which, for a second or two, resisted my efforts. "What should I see besides Aunt Reed in the apartment?—a man or a woman?" The handle turned, the door unclosed, and passing through and curtseying low, I looked up at—a black pillar!—such, at least, appeared to me, at first sight, the straight, narrow, sable-clad shape standing erect on the rug; the grim face at the top was like a carved mask, placed above the shaft by way of capital. . . .

"Your name, little girl?"

"Jane Eyre, sir."

In uttering these words I looked up: he seemed to me a tall gentleman, but then I was very little; his features were large,

The Miranda Complex

and they and all the lines of his frame were equally harsh and prim.[21]

That Jane does *not* function as the individualist locus of her own meaning and activity emerges from her indeterminate stance in this passage. She is afraid to return to the nursery, yet also afraid to enter the parlor; her only action is an "agitated hesitation" that in many ways recalls the interpretive ambiguity of Pomba Gira. In fact, what "decided me," that is, what provided the resolution to Jane's hesitation, originates externally rather than internally in the ringing of the breakfast-room bell. In contrast to the patriarchal I/eye who sees events as if in control of them, Jane's I/eye is powerless, passive, and stripped of its own self-determination.

At this point, the text makes a telling "cut" to the next paragraph, whose most extraordinary aspect is its framing of Brocklehurst in explicitly phallic terms: the black pillar standing erect (tumid penile shaft), whose grim face (glans) ejaculates the words (sperm) that engender "legitimate" meaning (biological and ideological patronymy). The significance of this context is underscored by the patriarchal conception of the phallus as whole, unitary, and simple and its corresponding perception of the vagina as chaotic and fragmented, or in filmic terms, the negative inverse of the masculine frame. The shot angle of Jane's—and consequently of the reader's—eye in this sequence is extremely revealing, for in contrast to high-angle shots that diminish the importance of the subject, low-angle shots emphasize the subject's power.[22] Jane's low-angle focus on Brocklehurst ("in uttering these words I looked up") articulates his power as both the subject of her discourse and the masculine Subject whose phallic presence implies her own castrated absence. Jane herself corroborates this pejorative positioning of women by describing how Brocklehurst, "bending from the perpendicular [flaccid after orgasm] . . . installed his person in the arm-chair." Just as Brocklehurst installs his person in Mrs. Reed's armchair, he textually installs a phallic Personhood over the castrated womanhood of Jane.

Jane Eyre's narrative cuts perform much the same role as the cuts of cinematic suture. Suture proceeds in the cinematic text through the joining of one shot to the next and comprises one of the most basic processes of that "compulsory and deliberate guidance of the thoughts and associations of the spectator" known as film editing.[23] Since the cut from one shot to the next guarantees that both preceding and subsequent shots will function as absences framing the meaning of the present, it also allows the cinematic text to be read as a signifying ensemble that converts one shot into both a signifier of the subsequent shot and the signified of the preceding one.[24] The cut described above "edits" the thoughts and associations of the reader into a similar signifying ensemble in which Jane's undecidability becomes a signifier of Brocklehurst as Phallus, and Brocklehurst as Phallus becomes the signified of Jane's undecidability. The ideological power of suture lies precisely in this editorial ability to reveal the absence of the castrated female in order to stitch over even more closely her temptation "to skid off-course, out-of-control, to prefer castration to false plenitude."[25] As a strategy of reading, it belies Spivak's description of Jane as the feminist individualist—an autonomous and fixed entity—and foregrounds her position as a "subject"— the product of signifying activities that are both culturally specific and generally unconscious.[26]

Perhaps the most characteristic filmic cut of suture is the shot/reverse shot formation, which establishes characters' optical points of view, especially in conversational settings.[27] No matter what the specific situation, the shot/reverse shot sequence invariably presents a shot of character A and a reverse shot of character B as seen by A, thus conforming the gaze of the viewer to that of character A as she looks at character B, and B as he looks at A. Consequently, the viewer must stand in for both characters, since neither A nor B appears in her or his respective reverse shots. However, as Jacqueline Rose notes in "Paranoia and the Film System," the shot/reverse shot formation betrays its own ambivalence by demanding that the viewer adopt a position in the reverse shot which directly contravenes that of the first.[28] For instance, Alfred Hitchcock's film *The Birds* encodes this contradiction into the text by placing the viewer first in the position of Melanie and then in that of the birds who attack her. Here, the editing procedure of suture speaks to its radically regressive potential, for it encourages a psychic operation that contravenes its larger signifying process.[29]

The Miranda Complex

If one accepts Kaja Silverman's suggestion in *The Subject of Semiotics* that first-person narration and all other point-of-view indicators are the novelistic equivalent of the filmic shot/reverse shot, then the scene between Jane and Brocklehurst also inscribes a subversive ambivalence, for it grants the reader an initial view of Jane and then a reverse view of Brocklehurst from Jane's perspective. Like the viewer of *The Birds*, the reader of *Jane Eyre* initially perceives Brocklehurst from the low-angle perspective of Melanie/plain Jane, and then Jane from the high-angle perspective of Brocklehurst, who seems just as malevolent as Hitchcock's murderous birds: "What a face he had . . . what a great nose! and what a mouth! and what large prominent teeth!" (*JE* 32). Although Little Red Riding Hood escaped the Big Bad Wolf, just as Jane ultimately escapes the wolfish Phallus of patriarchy, suture enables a resistant reading of Brontë's text by forcing the reader to live in the unsettling contradictions of Jane's subjectivity.

The relationship between Jane and Rochester expands the context of this sexual/textual war by demonstrating its particular tactics of insurgency. In her influential essay, "Visual Pleasure and Narrative Cinema," feminist filmmaker and critic Laura Mulvey observes that in the traditional exhibitionist role which patriarchal culture assigns to women, they are simultaneously looked at and displayed, and their appearance is coded for strong visual and erotic impact.[30] This feminine "to-be-looked-at-ness" transforms women into a fetish whose idealization fixates upon her physical beauty; thus, she becomes an object that satisfies rather than threatens impending castration. Such a fetishizing dynamic appears in dominant Hollywood cinema, for example, not only through the lingering close-ups that constitute woman as a spectacle but also through the glamorous costumes, makeup, settings, and lighting surrounding female stars.[31] That Rochester attempts to turn Jane into his own version of the female fetish seems irrefutable considering his premarital attempts to see her "glittering like a parterre" with jewels, satins, and silks; " 'I will make the world acknowledge you a beauty, too,' he went on, while I [Jane] really became uneasy at the strain he had adopted" (*JE* 261). Even on the most basic visual level, Jane's inability to satisfy the pleasure of the look, that is, the Phallic gaze, challenges the illusion of plenitude that Mulvey associates with classic narrative film; small, dark, and plain, a "heterogenous thing . . . a useless thing, incapable of serving their interest or adding to their pleasure" (*JE* 16), she cannot and will not focus the determining masculine gaze, whether of Rochester/Brocklehurst or of the viewing/reading subject.

In Jane's refusal of the look, she articulates a heterogenous discourse that aggressively insists upon its own castration—a fact that Nurse Bessie unwittingly acknowledges when she exclaims that Jane is a "little sharp thing" who had "got quite a new way of talking" (*JE* 40). The knifelike edges of Jane's discourse cut the chimerical threads suturing the wound of the subject together, and it is precisely this heterogenous sharpness that Althusserian interpellation blunts. Such a homogenizing tendency is exhibited, for example, by Catherine Belsey, whose work parallels Spivak's in that it borrows heavily from Althusser's theory of the text. According to Belsey, this process insures that the classic realist presentation of marriage often generates a new set of subject positions within the text that evoke closure and its concomitant qualities of order, definitiveness, and stability.[32] In her view, then, the marriage of Jane and Rochester would close off the threat to subjectivity and establish a unitary harmony within its new signifying relationships.[33] However, if one examines Jane and Rochester's marriage with a suturing eye rather than an interpellative "I," the subject positions generated fail to support Belsey's argument and illustrate the textual distortions that arise from an uncritical appropriation of Althusser.

The Madwoman in the Attic figures as centrally in the concealing processes of suture as she does in the address of interpellation, for the fire that Bertha sets severely impairs the scope of Rochester's determining masculine gaze and lays bare the extent of her own woundedness—her madness, imprisonment, and sexual rejection. However, the blindness that Rochester suffers as a result of Bertha's action paradoxically reverses the illusion of unity produced by suture—rather than concealing subjectivity, it prevents Rochester from the pleasure of "seeing" Jane, or any woman for that matter, as a fetishized object: " 'My seared vision! My crippled strength!' he murmured regretfully" (*JE* 449). Only when Rochester's inability to recognize others metamorphoses into a recognition of his own otherness does a marriage with Jane become possible: "It was mournful indeed, to witness the subjugation of that vigorous spirit. . . . He sat in his chair . . . the lines of now habitual sadness marking his strong features" (*JE* 444). Jane's narrative presence once again edits our sensibilities by directing them to the lines of the narrative frame. Unlike the "harsh" lines that Brocklehurst installed in the phallic chair of an imaginary omnipotence, Rochester's lines frame his position through partial vision and subjected impotence. The wounded "affirmities" of Rochester and Jane, then, and not the triumph of their imperialist and unitary identities, allow Jane to declare in that all too familiar line, "Reader, I married him."

Further, Spivak's claim that the "native" Bertha is sacrificed "as an insane animal for her sister's consolidation through marriage" (TWT 251) ignores the overdetermined nature of Jane's feminine "individualism," which does not exist as the "consolidation" or self-containment of masculine Selfhood but rather as a resistant autonomy forged in reaction against the ideological structures of patriarchy. Indeed, the text of *Jane Eyre* constructs a provocative scenario for this resistance: "I never can bear being dressed like a doll . . . or sitting like a second Danae with the golden shower falling daily round me. . . . He [Rochester] smiled; and I thought his smile was such as a sultan might, in a blissful and fond moment, bestow on a slave his gold and gems had enriched: I crushed his hand, which was ever hunting mine, vigorously, and thrust it back to him red with the passionate pressure" (*JE* 271). In this passage, Jane's sense of "annoyance and degradation" at Rochester's attempts to fetishize her are mediated through what she calls the "eastern illusion" and what I would call the rhetoric of historical imperialism. This rhetoric reveals the profound contradictions of Jane's position: while the ability to appropriate it as rhetoric irrevocably embeds her within the British imperialist project, her use of it as resistance to the masculinist and colonialist gaze simultaneously places her on the margins of imperialism. Interestingly, this image does not repeat the reductionist impulse of the woman=colonized, man=colonizer analogy within traditional feminist criticism, for its resolution—Jane's violent crushing of Rochester's hand—encourages the reader to draw contradictory parallels to the woman from the colonies rather than subsume her under a homogenous cross-referencing.

In order to explore these analogies, one must ask how a feminist reading can make the Invisible Woman—Bertha Mason—visible, especially since her suicide in *Jane Eyre* seems to cast her lot with all the other of our culture's politically "disappeared." In "Three Women's Texts," for example, Spivak comments that in the fictive England of *Jane Eyre*, Bertha must act out the transformation of her "self" into the Other, set fire to the house, and kill herself so that Jane might become the feminist individualist heroine of British fiction (TWT 251). She repeats her conflation of masculine and feminine subject positions by comparing the function of Bertha's death to *sati*, the Hindu ritual of burning widows alive on the funeral pyres of their husbands: "*Jane Eyre* can be read as the orchestration and staging of the self-immolation of Bertha Mason as 'good wife'" (TWT 259). Or, Bertha—the good wife— sacrifices herself for the good of her husband—the white (fe)male. Spivak's attempt to expand the frontiers of the politics of reading not only falls short in its portrayal of the particular oppression of women but also, by characterizing Bertha only as a victim, fails to detect a far more subversive politics embedded within her violent act. Like Jane, Bertha Mason will "not be hurried away in a suttee" (*JE* 275).

At first glance, it seems difficult to posit any direct meaning for Bertha's suicide since we only hear of it secondhand, through the butler's eyewitness account as recounted by Jane. This narrative remoteness from Bertha's death seems to parallel Gilbert and Gubar's erasure of her life, for both deny us access to the independent reality of the woman from the colonies. However, if we locate Bertha's act within the larger context of women's suicide, a counter-reading emerges that grants Bertha an integrity absent in both Gilbert and Gubar's and Spivak's construction of her. In a study of women and madness that remains provocative in spite of its fifteen-year publication lapse, Phyllis Chesler notes that "men commit actions; women commit gestures. . . . 'Manfully,' men kill themselves, or others—*physically*. Women *attempt* to kill themselves physically far more often than men do, and fail at it more often. Suicide is not an apolitical occurrence."[34] Because physical action—even the self-destructive action of taking one's own life—is very difficult for women, they tend more toward psychic and emotional self-destruction.[35] Female suicide attempts function not so much as calls for help as "the assigned baring of the powerless throat, *signals of ritual readiness for self-sacrifice*" (emphasis added).[36] Chesler's analysis of women's suicide attempts as a sign of their powerlessness and psychological martyrdom seems very close to Spivak's description of Bertha's death as a sign of the ritual self-sacrifice necessary when women become *sati*.

However, the fact that Bertha commits rather than attempts suicide moves her into a very different position from the one just described. According to Chesler, women who succeed at taking their own lives outwit and reject their "feminine" role at the only price possible: their deaths. We do not know what Bertha shouted at Rochester before she leaped from Thornfield's roof, but we can conjecture that her insistence upon the violent physical destruction of both Thornfield and herself constitutes an act of resistance not only to her status as a woman in a patriarchal culture but also as a colonized object. That this interpretation of Bertha exists at least implicitly within the text is supported by Alexander Baron's meticulously faithful dramatization of *Jane Eyre* for the BBC. In his screenplay, Bertha (Joolia Cappelman) sensationally leaps to her death—but not before she faces Rochester (Timothy Dalton) and screams: "I hate you! I hate you!"

This direct encounter between oppressed and oppressor grants Bertha's self-destructive act a defiant subversiveness that always lurks at the edges of Brontë's text. In his study, *Frantz Fanon and the Psychology of Oppression*, Hussein Abdilahi Bulhan comments that colonialism requires that the colonized deeply fear their own biological death, for the fear of physical death hinders not only the possibility of freedom but also productive and meaningful living.[37] Those who submit to oppression may continue to breathe, eat, and sleep; "unfortunately, however, they only exchange one form of death for another. This is so because as they submit to oppression and preserve biological life, they invariably suffer a degree of *psychological* and *social* death."[38] Indeed, he states, the more the oppressed seek physical survival, the more their oppression deepens. It seems quite plausible, then, that Bertha's self-imposed death tragically asserts resistance rather than defeat and provides a presence that counters the invisibility imposed upon her both by Gilbert and Gubar's hermeneutics of suspicion and by Spivak's contention that she dies on the pyre of feminist individualism.

It is in this context of resistance that one could argue for Jane and Bertha as oppressed rather than opposed sisters. Both are imprisoned by the textual figure who represents patriarchal imperialism (Jane psychologically, Bertha physically), and both resist their imprisonment with violent gestures (Jane symbolically crushes him and Bertha literally immolates his patronymy). Not surprisingly, these parallels break down under the weight of the fact that Jane lives to experience a positive catharsis of her imprisonment, while Bertha's catharsis demands that she die. At the very least, however, they require us to relinquish the quest for univocity—whether of masculine subject and feminine object or of colonizer and colonized. Plain Jane's heterogenous absence and Bertha's insistent presence maim this will to unity with a visible wound that we can neither suture over nor erase within the white(fe)male palimpsest.

2

The King and I in Uncle Tom's Cabin; or, On the Borders of the Women's Room

Works are . . . not autonomous systems, "organic wholes," but intertextual constructs: sequences which have meaning in relation to other texts which they take up, cite, parody, refute, or generally transform. A text can be read only in relation to other texts, and it is made possible by the codes which animate the discursive space of a culture.
Jonathan Culler, In Pursuit of Signs

I think the white man's model will impose itself on us whether we like it or not. And soon the world will belong to those who know how to make use of it.
Babatunde Traore in Maryse Conde's Segu

"Mira was hiding out in the ladies' room. She called it that, even though someone had scratched out the word *ladies'* in the sign on the door, and written *women's* underneath."[1] Mira, of course, is the first character we meet in *The Women's Room*, Marilyn French's 1977 feminist magnum opus. She is hiding out in the ladies' room because at Harvard in 1968, it is one of the few gendered spaces allotted to women—"the school had been planned for men, and there were places, she had been told, where women were simply not permitted to go" (*WR* 10). In the decade since French's novel, however, the women's movement has transformed this image of woman marginalized within her assigned space into one that celebrates the difference of the "women's room." The explosive growth of such women-only phenomena as consciousness-raising groups, the woman-church, women's caucuses within the academic disciplines, Women's Studies programs, feminist journal and media collectives, and women's music festivals testifies to the psychological and social importance of creating spaces where women's difference from men can be affirmed, analyzed, and verified.[2] Further, as Teresa de Lauretis notes in *Technologies of Gender: Essays on Theory, Film, and Fiction*, these gendered havens greatly expanded feminism's political arsenal because they helped women resist the Patriarchal Imperative, that is, the morally and legally institutionalized masculine demand of unlimited access to women: "Female denial of male access to females substantially cuts off a flow of benefits, but it has also the form and full portent of assumption of power."[3]

Feminism's visit to the women's room has encouraged the articulation of gender as sexual difference and given birth to numerous theories supporting the notion of a distinctly female perspective: gynocriticism (Elaine Showalter), maternal thinking (Sara Ruddick), and feminine writing (Hélène Cixous). Yet this concept of gender as sexual difference also works to disempower feminist thought to the extent that it constructs a universalized woman and reifies her difference from a universalized man (*TOG* 2). Defining women in terms of their difference from men actually prevents an adequate critique because it distorts race and class differences not only among women but also *within* women (*TOG*

2). According to de Lauretis, feminists cannot explain "differences among women who wear the veil, women who 'wear the mask' (a metaphor by Paul Lawrence Dunbar often quoted by black women writers) and women who masquerade (Joan Riviere)" by appealing solely to sexual difference: "From that point of view, they would not be differences at all, and all women would but render either different embodiments of some archetypal essence of woman, or more or less sophisticated impersonations of a metaphysical-discursive femininity" (TOG 2).

Recent work both by women of color and by white women has attempted to dismantle this metaphysical-discursive femininity by uncovering the race and class differences that exist among the world's extremely diverse communities of women. It seems much harder, however, to grasp how such differences work *within* women and to theorize an ideology of gender that captures the fluidity and complexity of what we call "identity." For example, describing the position of a white, middle-class woman either as oppressed or oppressive might vary in terms of her racial or economic status; indeed, she can sometimes be both simultaneously— in a patriarchal society, her femaleness dictates her subjection as sexual object, and in a racist society, her whiteness dictates her often unwitting participation in sustaining a system of white supremacy. Another way of saying this is that sometimes women can be in the men's room and not even know it.

A brilliant example of how to conceptualize this difference *within* women emerges from one of the most popular musical films of the last forty years—Rodgers and Hammerstein's *The King and I* (1956), which chronicles the adventures of English governess Mrs. Anna Leonowens (Deborah Kerr) at the Siamese court.[4] This film, perhaps the greatest success of all the Rodgers and Hammerstein stage-to-screen productions, boasts a long and intricately woven intertextual lineage: it adapts Rodgers and Hammerstein's 1951 Broadway play of the same name, which adapts Talbot Jennings and Sally Benson's 1945 screenplay of *Anna and the King of Siam* (with Irene Dunne and Rex Harrison as Anna and the King), which adapts Margaret Landon's 1944 novel, *Anna and the King of Siam*, which adapts Mrs. Leonowens's diaries.

Clearly, this narrative of a young widow whose pluck and determination enabled her to care for her young son and Westernize a proud Asian monarch captured the Anglo-American cultural imagination like no other story during the post–World War II era.

In order to explore "Mrs. Anna's" contradictory ideological positioning, however, a feminist analysis must move beyond (but not discard) an "images of women" approach that emphasizes the contextual portrayal of plot and character. Since the Rodgers and Hammerstein film germinated from Mrs. Anna Leonowens's real-life diaries, *The English Governess at the Siamese Court: Being Recollections of Six Years in the Royal Palace at Bangkok* (1870) and *Siamese Harem Life* (1873), its artifice necessarily includes the historical context of the politics of empire and England's colonization of India in the latter half of the nineteenth century. In his extensive study *Empires*, Michael Doyle observes that "empires are relationships of political control over a people. . . . Control exists in and is defined by its behavioral effects on those who are controlled. It is this control which must be explained."[5] While Doyle is specifically referring to socioeconomic relations, his definition also includes those less tangible processes of colonialism that affect the way we construct ideologies—especially ideologies of gender.

A detailed reading of these myriad rewritings of Mrs. Leonowens's story and the relationships of political control that they exert upon each other will reveal the clues necessary to solve the ideological riddle of "Mrs. Anna's" oppressed and oppressive participation in the Anglo-European imperial project. This reading will also enable us to excavate the intersections of race, gender, and class that inhabit not only the particular position of Anna in *The King and I* but also the general position of white, middle-class women. We will discover that along with the feminist whose explicit dialogue resists oppression, there exists a woman whose cinematic presence holds and maintains the masculinist gaze; along with the fiery abolitionist who disseminates *Uncle Tom's Cabin* in order to subvert slavery, there exists a woman who, through this very dissemination, imprisons Siamese women within an ethnocentric vision of angelic motherhood; and along with the critical anti-imperialist, there exists a woman whose zeal to liberate legitimates the agendas of a colonialist society.

The first clue to the riddle of Anna—her feminism—existed only implicitly in the play's original theatrical run but was emphasized explicitly in its highly successful 1976 revival on Broadway. Yul Brynner, who reprised his role as King Mongkut, affirmed the importance of Anna's stubborn advocacy of social and political rights for women when he remarked to the *New York Times* that "the play has become more contemporary than it was in 1951, when it first opened. Oscar Hammerstein 2nd, who wrote the book and the lyrics . . . touched on many things, such as the right of a woman to have her condition respected. . . . The values were there all the time, but they were then an intellectual concept. Today, human rights are a part of everyday life."[6] For Anna, feminism and the right of a woman to have her condition respected entailed a journey to the women's room, for she demands nothing less than twenty pounds a month and a house of her own outside the palace walls.

Such a demand sounds remarkably similar to Virginia Woolf's prescription for women of five hundred pounds a year and a room of one's own. For Woolf, the curative benefits of this medicine include "the urbanity, the geniality, the dignity which are the offspring of luxury and privacy and space"[7]—all of which the narrator of Woolf's essay, *A Room of One's Own*, gains when her Aunt Mary Beton suffers a fatal fall while taking the air in Bombay. (It is curious that feminists have not on the whole been troubled by *how* Aunt Mary Beton's money was made, especially given its "context" of the English colonization of India.) Margaret Landon's novel portrays Anna as clearly agreeing with Woolf, for "it was important to establish her position at once, and her right to respect and privacy were integral parts of that."[8] It is precisely this feisty insistence on her privacy and rights that the Rodgers and Hammerstein film appropriates and that comprises a major portion of its antisexist stance.

In one very early scene, for example, the women of the Nang Harm, or Royal Harem, persist in calling Anna "sir." When she asks why, Lady Thiang, King Mongkut's senior wife, responds:

Lady Thiang: Because you scientific. Not lowly, like woman.
Anna: Do you *all* think women are more lowly than men?
(The women nod their heads in happy agreement.)
Anna (indignantly): Well, I don't!
Lady Thiang: Please sir, do not tell King. Make King angry.
Anna: Perhaps it's time someone did tell him a thing or two.[9]

Because this exchange occurs in the opening scenes of the film, it strongly encourages us to notice both the content of Anna's assertion, which establishes women's inalienable claim to dignity, and her assertiveness, which contravenes the traditional stereotype of women as irrational and submissive.

However, *The King and I* also subverts this feminism by colonizing Anna as just another patriarchal object. The enabling conditions of this subversion reside within the cinematic textuality of the film itself, since it constructs Anna as subject not only through the unfolding narrative but also by those material practices—such as point-of-view shots—that make *The King and I* visible to the spectator. French cinematographer Robert Bresson identifies one of the most important of these material practices in his observation that "to set up a film is to bind persons to each other and to objects by looks."[10] Directors often establish this chain of gazes through "subjective" point-of-view shots, which conflate the lens of the camera with the eye of the spectator and bring her into an intentional relationship with the filmic material.

Feminist film critics such as Laura Mulvey and E. Ann Kaplan have described this process as the "complex gaze apparatus" of classical Hollywood cinema, which objectifies women characters on the screen and women spectators off the screen. It objectifies these women because the act of "gazing" both constructs and depends upon sexual difference: through male characters gazing at female characters, who then become objects of the gaze; through spectators, whose perspectival identification with the camera also brings them into relationship with its masculinist gaze; and through the camera, whose very act of filming is predominantly controlled by men.[11] In terms of a film's relationships of political control, then, classical cinema often colonizes its female characters and spectators through the perspectival chains forged within a gaze apparatus that defines men as the bearer and women as the object of the filmic "look."

Although Mulvey's articulation of spectatorial ideology has been much discussed and revised over the last decade,[12] its basic assumptions are still valid for *The King and I*, which places Anna the feminist in the position of the woman who "holds the look, plays to and signifies male desire."[13] Anna's status as object of the look is most vividly revealed during a dinner and subsequent performance of *Uncle Tom's Cabin* arranged for the entertainment of the visiting English diplomats. In the initial shot of this sequence, King Mongkut sexualizes Anna's presence by remarking upon the daringly low-cut dress she wears—a sexualization that the camera perpetuates by conflating itself with the King's lingering inspection of Anna's bare shoulders and her pronounced cleavage. Since our spectatorial vision follows that of the camera, this point-of-view shot sexualizes our own perception of Anna as well. This cinematic coding of her appearance for strong visual and erotic impact—or, in Mulvey's terms, her "to-be-looked-at-ness"—fetishizes Anna and uncovers the asymmetries of power lurking in *The King and I*'s material practices. In actuality, the King (here, representative of patriarchy) controls the look, but the content of the film tricks us into believing that Anna controls her own feminine/feminist vision.

Anna's objectification by the patriarchal gaze intensifies after the dinner, when she relives the anxiety-ridden excitement of her first schoolgirl dance by waltzing around the ballroom and bursting into the song, "Shall We Dance?" The master script provides the context for this shot sequence when it notes that "Anna, carried away by her reminiscent mood, dances around the ballroom until she glides by the King and realizes that he is looking at her very much as he might look at one of his dancing girls. She stops" (KI 93). Embarrassed and confused, Anna attempts to redirect the King's gaze and, by implication, the gaze of the camera: "Your Majesty, I—I didn't realize I was—after all, I'm not a dancing girl. In England, we don't—that is, a girl would not dance while a man is looking at her" (KI 93).

In her seminal essay "Visual Pleasure and Narrative Cinema,"

Mulvey observes that the showgirl allows a film technically to unite the gaze constructing woman as an erotic object for the characters with that constructing her as an erotic object for the spectators, with no break in its diegesis: "A woman performs within the narrative, the gaze of the spectator and that of the male characters in the film are neatly combined without breaking narrative verisimilitude." [14] *The King and I* accomplishes this unification not only through Anna's temporary assumption of the showgirl's persona but also through its material practices as cinematic text. During much of Anna's dance, for example, the King remains physically off scene; the camera, however, inscribes his presence within the shot by conforming its vision to that of the King watching Anna. Our spectatorial gaze forms the third element of this triangle, since we look at Anna through the camera's—and thus the King's—eyes.

The tension between *The King and I*'s contextual liberation and textual colonization of Anna becomes even more significant when it embeds this contradiction within a theatrical performance of *Uncle Tom's Cabin*. In her own "Siamese version of famous American book," Tuptim (a very young Rita Moreno) enthralls the dinner's English guests and amply demonstrates King Mongkut's "civility." Indeed, it is this insertion of Harriet Beecher Stowe's immensely popular abolitionist work into *The King and I*'s text that raises profound questions about the filmic intersections of race and gender—a fact that does not seem surprising given Anna's own real-life conversion to abolitionism through her reading of *Uncle Tom*.[15] *Uncle Tom's Cabin* becomes an ideological locus of the film when, immediately after Anna's declaration of women's equality to the Nang Harm (Royal Harem), Tuptim asks for an English book to read; several scenes later, we discover that Stowe's novel is the very book which Anna lends Tuptim. In an extremely clever intertextual twist, then, cinema uses the novel to bind the rights of women to the rights of slaves, for as a gift from the Prince of Burma to the King of Siam, Tuptim figures the oppression of both.

In many ways, one might think *The King and I* extraordinarily prescient for its recognition of *Uncle Tom*'s importance years before its rehabilitation within feminist circles. Ridiculed by critics for its "feminine" sentimentality and excluded from the canon of "great" American works, *Uncle Tom* exemplifies perhaps more than any other text the agenda of the (predominantly male) literary establishment. And, more than any other text, its reclamation has furnished feminist criticism with a highly visible cause célèbre since many have argued that its exclusion from the canon was no accident. As Jane Tompkins contends in her essay "Sentimental Power: *Uncle Tom's Cabin* and the Politics of Literary History," Stowe's novel "represents a monumental effort to reorganize culture from the women's point of view. . . . Out of the ideological materials they had at their disposal, the sentimental novelists elaborated a myth that gave women the central position of power and authority in the culture; and of these efforts *Uncle Tom's Cabin* is the most dazzling exemplar." [16] Further, according to Tompkins, Stowe's text functions as a means of both describing and changing the social world: its reinforcement of a particular code of values not only offers a strategy for dealing with the cultural conflict over slavery but also practices the very measures it prescribes (SP 91).

Of course, the code of values that *Uncle Tom* reinforces is the nineteenth-century ideology of the "moral mother," whose innate patience, piety, and compassion become the model for all social change. In Stowe's novel, these qualities certainly characterize the Quakeress Rachel Halliday, in whose morally maternal arms a fleeing George and Eliza find comfort, and upon whose forehead "time had written no inscription, except peace on earth, good will to men." [17] It seems especially apt that Stowe situates the reader's first glimpse of Rachel in that most traditional of all women's rooms—the kitchen: "A large, roomy, neatly-painted kitchen, its yellow floor glossy and smooth, and without a particle of dust; a neat, well-blacked cooking-stove; rows of shining tins, suggestive of unmentionable good things to the appetite . . . a rocking-chair . . . motherly and old, whose wide arms breathed hospitable invitation" (*UTC* 214).

According to Tompkins, Stowe attempts nothing less than a transformation of American society through a mother's redemptive love and the relocation of sociopolitical power from the jurisdiction of law, marketplace, and government to that of women's domestic sphere: "Centering on the home, for these women, is not a way of indulging in narcissistic fantasy, as critics have argued, or a turning away from the world into self-absorption and idle reverie; it is the prerequisite of world conquest, defined as the reformation of the human race through proper care and nurturing of its young" (SP 98). Yet by leaving the moral mother and her "blueprint for colonizing the world" locked, so to speak, in the kitchen, both Stowe and brilliant feminist critics such as Tompkins fail to acknowledge how this important and necessary revaluation of women's (white, middle-class) culture becomes complicitous with oppressive ideologies of race and class.

Such complicity becomes most evident in Stowe's presentation of the slave Eliza, who flees to Canada in order to prevent kind "Mas'r Shelby" from selling her young son. While Eliza's escape certainly describes the experience of some female slaves, historical evidence suggests that far fewer females than males resisted slavery by running away. More common female patterns of resistance include psychological warfare, pilfering, and poisoning as well as abortion and infanticide.[18] It is in fact the bitter (and atheist) quadroon Cassy, rather than the gentle (and Christian) Eliza, who employs the much more probable gender-specific strategies of black women's struggle against slavery.

Cassy's euthanasia of her infant son by an overdose of laudanum, her threat to poison her master Simon Legree, and her ultimate defeat of Legree by a cunning exploitation of his guilt and belief in ghosts beg the question of why Stowe, *The King and I*, and Tompkins, for that matter, focus predominantly upon Eliza and Little Eva—two women molded from the same pattern of angelic motherhood. One ready answer comes from Stowe herself, who claimed to have created Eliza as a sympathetic black moral mother with whom *Uncle Tom*'s majority of white readers could easily identify. Yet I believe that this rationale obscures the way in which Stowe's novel recuperates the far more threatening character of Cassy through Eliza's reassuring maternity and, in so doing, enacts perhaps the most destructive and pervasive form of colonialist domination—the reduction of the Other (black, female, and enslaved) to the same (white, middle-class, and morally maternal).

The King and I in Uncle Tom's Cabin

Michel de Certeau comments in *Heterologies: Discourse on the Other* that "it is ideologically inconceivable that there should exist an otherness of the same ontological status as the same, without there being immediately mounted an effort at its appropriation."[19] Angela Davis invests de Certeau's statement with a concrete political content when she argues that "the central female figure [in *Uncle Tom's Cabin*] is a travesty of the Black woman, a naive transposition of the mother-figure, praised by the cultural propaganda of the period, from white society to the slave community. Eliza is white motherhood incarnate, but in blackface."[20] Motivated by a passionate hatred of slavery, black women did not receive their strength through a mystical devotion to the umbilical cord but rather forged it through the crucible of their concrete historical experience as slaves. At this point, the socionarrative space of *Uncle Tom's Cabin* seems dangerously close to the "Uncle Tom's Cabin" that Frederick Douglass describes as Stowe's own dwelling place in Andover, Massachusetts: it was "an edifice, by the way, bearing little resemblance to slave cabins."[21]

Like her mentor Stowe, Mrs. Anna Leonowens also desired to resurrect the values of angelic motherhood within the women of the harem, for "in the brutal tragedy of a slave's experience,—a female slave in the harem of an Asian despot,—the native angel in her had been bruised, mutilated, defaced, deformed, but not quite obliterated."[22] This statement expresses a very common sympathetic stance that "First World" women adopt toward their "Third World" sisters. However, the problems underlying this attitude of sisterhood surface in Leila Ahmed's study of Western ethnocentrism and perceptions of the harem. Ahmed suggests that while Western feminists—much like Anna—have succeeded in rejecting myths about the innate inferiority of (Western) women, they continue to perpetuate those myths about women sequestered in harems: "To conceive of us as existing mindlessly passive, indifferent, perhaps unaware of our oppression, tolerating a situation no Western woman would tolerate . . . is to assume, and imply, our 'inferiority.'"[23]

In fact, the nine thousand women of King Mongkut's palace possessed far more political and economic power than Anna and, indeed, than most Anglo-European women during that historical period. They passed their own laws and settled disputes before female judges. Further, as Anna records, they supported their own prisons, markets, merchants, brokers, teachers, and mechanics of every kind and degree—"and every function of every nature is exercised by women, and by them only."[24] While women could enter the palace to serve their men, no man could enter the harem except the king. An inviolable women's room, the harem enclosed a gendered space that enabled women to congregate freely and exchange ideas and information without interference from men.[25] It becomes difficult, then, to accept uncritically Anna's view of the Nang Harm women as brutally enslaved and oppressed, and one must ask why she, as well as many Western feminists, believe that women secluded and barred from the company of men are necessarily deprived.[26]

Anna's discourse of the harem conceals a speaking position (her own), from which power-knowledge is exercised, and a spoken subject (the women of the Nang Harm), which is brought into existence through the exercise of power-knowledge.[27] These respective positions are revealed in the depiction of Anna's mission in Landon's novel, *Anna and the King of Siam*: "Perhaps the opportunity to teach in the harem meant that she would be able to inculcate into her pupils her own deep sense of the sacredness of the human soul, and the evil of any system which violated it by permitting one person to own another" (*AK* 40). The most revealing portion of this passage is the choice of the verb "inculcate" to describe the action, for its etymology (from the Latin verb *inculcare*) connotes a trampling in as well as an impressing upon—a linguistic and cultural heritage that rigorously interrogates Anna's project of liberation through education.

In his *Pedagogy of the Oppressed*, Paulo Freire echoes de Certeau's characterization of colonialism as the reduction of the Other to the same when he identifies the prescriptive mentality as one of the most basic elements in the relationship between oppressor and oppressed. This prescriptiveness imposes one human's choice upon another and brings the consciousness of the one prescribed to into conformity with that of the prescriber.[28] Anna's individual sense of manifest destiny—her desire to instill within her pupils the "higher" spiritual laws—exemplifies this process because it forges a Westernized humanitarian sensibility *for* rather than *with* the oppressed. As Freire observes, "No pedagogy which is truly liberating can remain distant from the oppressed . . . by presenting for their emulation models from among the oppressors"; to do so makes objects of the oppressed, and these prescriptive models become the instrument of their dehumanization.[29]

Anna unwittingly convicts herself on these grounds by admitting that she was "not someone who could fight with guns to free the slaves, as in the United States, but someone who could fight with knowledge in the corner of the world where she found herself" (*AK* 82). For her, the transmission of superior cultural values and an unassailable knowledge of the Nang Harm women as "brutally enslaved" becomes a weapon just as powerful as a gun. With the best of feminist and anti-imperialist intentions, then, Anna's educational mission resonates with the larger pattern of England's colonialist domination, which tended to leave a country's ruling elite intact and to achieve social, political, and economic hegemony through indirect means.

Susantha Goontilake notes in her study *Crippled Minds: An Exploration into Colonial Culture* that Macaulay and his fellow British colonials in India hoped that the importation of English education would weaken the hold of indigenous cultural and religious traditions and create the space for the inculcation of Anglo-European values.[30] To facilitate this ethnic subversion, they developed what one could only call a "trickle-down" theory of English colonialism: by using education to convert the ruling elite, Macaulay and friends hoped to create a deeply entrenched process of autocolonization through which Indians would internalize and disseminate the values of Queen Victoria's England. It is within this framework that the specter of Anna's double-voicedness returns to haunt her, for it articulates her resistance to, yet complicity with, England's imperialist agenda.

However, like Stowe's novel, the *Uncle Tom's Cabin* of *The King and I* enacts its own strategies of resistance by providing both the thematic and cinematic moment of Eliza/Tuptim's escape from slavery. This represents a significant rewriting of Mrs. Leonowens's diaries and Margaret Landon's novel, for in both, it is Lady Son Klin—imprisoned for collaborating with the

French—who not only translates *Uncle Tom* into Siamese but also adopts Stowe's name as her own. Performed in *The King and I* as entertainment after the diplomatic dinner, the "Small House of Uncle Thomas" transforms *Uncle Tom's Cabin* from a theatrical demonstrating King Mongkut's "civility" to one that challenges his patriarchal and monarchical ownership of women and slaves: the evil Simon Legree metamorphoses into King Mongkut, and the fleeing Eliza, into Tuptim herself. The shooting script of the film reinforces our perception of this metamorphosis by directing the camera to cut at strategic moments to the King who, the script declares, scowls with increasing severity at the rebelliousness of Tuptim's message (KI 82).

One of *The King and I*'s most powerful vehicles for framing the thematic moment of escape is its insertion of culturally coded written texts, that is, its intertextuality. We have already seen how the insertion of *Uncle Tom's Cabin* "Westernizes" the film's concept of freedom, and I would argue that a similar insertion—this time, of the biblical Exodus story—buttresses Tuptim's insurgency by implying its theological mandate. Immediately before the diplomatic fete and the performance of *Uncle Tom's Cabin*, the King hands Anna a note listing all the topics he would like to elaborate upon during dinner—the most important of which is the topic of Moses. Anna complies with the King's request by remarking to his guests: "His Majesty made a rather interesting point about Moses the other day when he was reading the Bible" (KI 78). While Anna's remark seems charmingly innocuous, it actually possesses an extremely important cinematic function: suturing the film's external audience into the position of its internal one.

In *The Hollywood Musical*, Jane Feuer notes that the musical often put theatrical audiences into a film for the purpose of shaping the responses of its movie audience.[31] *The King and I* uses its theatrical audience for a similar purpose: shaping the response of its external audience through a perspectival chain like the one that positions Anna as the object of the look. For example, the spectator sees Anna (seated directly to the King's left) and hears the remark about Moses from the position of a dinner guest several seats away. This conflation of external with internal audience continues during the performance of *Uncle Tom's Cabin* through the camera's adoption of a traditional third row center perspective and its subsequent cut to a closer shot of the performance. As Feuer remarks: "In this second shot (or more properly in the effect of the cut to this shot) the spectator replaces the internal audience. The subjectivity of the spectator stands in for that of the spectral audience."[32] Since the internal audience of the "Small House of Uncle Thomas" consists entirely of British dignitaries and local officials sympathetic to England, the film tightly sutures our spectatorial subjectivity to that body of Anglo-European values whose dissemination Macaulay thought so important to preventing the sun from ever setting on Victoria's empire.

Ironically, it is this intrusion of the internal audience between spectator and performance that endows us with the effect of living—indeed, *sharing*—a film experience.[33] In this case, the "shared" experience of Moses—like our experience of Anna's feminism—evokes the Western ideology of human rights and invites us to draw parallels between Moses' liberation of the slaves in Egypt, the liberation of Eliza in *Uncle Tom's Cabin*, and Tuptim's liberation from the palace of the King. The "Siamese version of famous American book" accommodates such parallels by reworking Stowe's plot with the heavy hand of divine intervention. Eliza's escape now witnesses to the nonhuman miracles of Buddha (who, in this instance, seems identical to the Jewish/Christian God) rather than the very human activity of the Underground Railroad.

Even the miracles that the deity of the "Small House of Uncle Thomas" uses to liberate the captives and annihilate the oppressors duplicate those of the Exodus story: just as the biblical Yahweh parts the Red Sea so that Moses and the Israelites might escape Pharaoh, Buddha freezes the great river to provide a safe path for Eliza; just as Yahweh drowns Pharaoh and his armies by a tidal surge as they try to cross the sea, Buddha sends the sun that melts the ice and drowns the evil Simon Legree and his "scientific" hunting dogs; and just as the Israelites joyously celebrate their freedom by singing praises to God, Eliza and friends celebrate their freedom by singing praises to Buddha. At the end of the play, Tuptim makes the parallel between herself and Eliza explicit when she steps out of her role as narrator to address the

King directly: "I too am glad for death of King. Of any king who pursues Slave who is unhappy and tries to escape!" (KI 83).

While this transference of a highly subversive social plot from one universe of discourse—Christian abolitionism—to another —Buddhist monarchism—might seem revolutionary, it becomes much more questionable when one compares Anna's own narration of Tuptim's escape in her diaries with its function as cinematic signifier in *The King and I*. In *Siamese Harem Life*, Tuptim plots her own escape by shaving off her hair and disguising herself as a male priest. After running away from the harem, she hides by taking refuge in the monastery of the Rajah Bah ditt Sang and becoming a disciple of P'hra Balat, who was once her promised husband: "Then P'hra Balat took me to his cell; but he did not recognize in the young priest I seemed to be the Tuptim he had known in his boyhood, and who had once been his betrothed wife" (*SHL* 24). Tuptim grows in wisdom under the tutelage of her former betrothed and soon acknowledges that this spiritual serenity far surpasses the ephemeral transience of any sexual relationship. The discovery of her disguise, however, leads to the arrest of both disciple and master, even though no sexual malfeasance has occurred. This Tuptim endures her capture and subsequent burning at the stake in a starkly heroic manner, eliciting a stunned response by Anna:

> I [Anna] sat stupefied at the transformation that had been wrought in the Tuptim I had known. Her hair was cut close to her head, and her eyebrows had been shaved off. Her cheeks were hollow and sunken. Her eyes were cast down. Her hands were manacled, and her bare little feet could hardly drag along the heavy chains that were fastened to her ankles. . . . Her whole form was still childlike, but she held herself erect, and her manner was self-possessed. When she spoke, her voice was clear and vibrating, her accent firm and unflinching. . . . She made no obeisance, no humble, appealing prostration. (*SHL* 22)

Anna's recognition of Tuptim's strength contrasts with the character bearing the same name in *The King and I*, and no instance evidences this more clearly than the cinematic moment of Tuptim's escape. The Hammerstein/Lehman screenplay insures that viewers perceive the parallel between Tuptim and Eliza by situating her escape literally in the interstice between the end of the "Small House of Uncle Thomas" and the resumption of the film proper. During the curtain calls, Tuptim seizes the moment to meet her forbidden Burmese lover, Lun Tha, who has engineered their elopement together. Perhaps the shot that most vividly captures the difference between the Tuptim of Anna's diaries and of *The King and I* is the one framing our final glimpse of the hapless young lovers: Tuptim passive and invisible in the rickshaw pulled by an active and visible Lun Tha.

Because it invests Tuptim's escape with the context of unrequited love rather than hatred of oppression, *The King and I* not only recuperates the heroism of the woman in *Siamese Harem Life* but also calls into question the liberatory parallels of *Uncle Tom's Cabin* with the Exodus story. Liberation—for women, anyway—becomes less a struggle for political and social freedom than a desperate desire to be with the man you love. Unlike Anna's character, the Tuptim of Hammerstein/Lehman encourages us to define her as a helpless victim by frantically begging for mercy and prostrating herself in terror. Such a presentation enmeshes Tuptim within patriarchal notions of women's subordination to men and privileges an ideology of the Westernized romantic couple. Although Malek Alloula addresses the French colonization of Algeria, the criticism he makes could easily apply to *The King and I*'s interpretation of Tuptim's story: "The couple, in the Western sense, is an aberration, a historical error, an unthinkable possibility. . . . The representation of the couple is the expression of a double symbolic violence perpetrated on Algerian society: it rearranges its space and its structure on the basis of alien criteria."[34] One could argue that if Anna remodels the women's room according to the blueprint of angelic motherhood, then *The King and I* redecorates it with phallocentric and ethnocentric motifs of romance.

Tuptim's escape also foregrounds Anna's contradictory social positioning through her response to the King's "monstrous" and "inhuman" refusal to free the young woman and his insistence upon punishing her—an attitude Anna finds so shocking that in her memoirs she recalls fainting, or perhaps more accurately, lapsing into cultural unconsciousness. In a very interesting way, this act duplicates the Oriental scene that *The English Governess at the Siamese Court* initially presents to readers and that *The King and I* appropriates for its viewers: the situation "was as Oriental as the scene—heartless arbitrary insolence on the part of my employers; homelessness, forlornness, helplessness, mortification, indignation, on mine" (*EG* 10).

The King and I uses almost identical language to present Anna's confrontation with King Mongkut about Tuptim's punishment. Angry that the King intends to have Tuptim flogged, Anna provokes the following dialogue:

> Anna: This girl hurt your vanity, that's all! She didn't hurt your heart! You haven't got a heart! You've never loved anyone! You never will!
> King (deeply hurt, he must hurt Anna in return): I show you! Give! Give to me! (he snatches a whip from the guard and cracks it over Tuptim's head).
> Anna (horrified): I can't believe you're going to do this dreadful thing!
> King: You do not believe, eh? Maybe you believe when you hear her screaming as you run from here!
> Anna: I am not going to run! I am going to stand right here and watch you!
> King (to the guards): Hold this girl! I do this all myself!
> Anna: You *are* a barbarian! (KI 99)

As Anna delivers the last remark with the proper amount of righteous indignation, the camera punctuates its importance with a close-up of her face and upper body rigid with sincerity and passion. What concerns me about this characterization is Anna's arrogance and blindness in construing difference as the Nonhuman Other. In this respect, both the autobiographical and filmic texts we have considered reproduce what Aimé Cesaire calls in his *Discourse on Colonialism* "the dishonest equations *Christianity=civilization, paganism=savagery*, from which there could not but ensue abominable colonialist and racist consequences."[35]

The King and I in Uncle Tom's Cabin

The contradiction of an Anglo-European woman whose moving witness to the courage and oppression of her sisters simultaneously colonizes them in the name of "humanity" profoundly captures some of the complexities of current feminist debates about such practices as *sati* (the ritual suicide of Hindu widows) or clitoridectomy (surgical removal of the clitoris). While no one would or should defend Tuptim's wrongful execution—or *sati*, for that matter—the decisions leading to this end do not necessarily represent an amoral chaos but rather a system of laws embodying profound differences in English and Siamese perceptions of society, the individual, and the idea of justice. We might protest those laws; however, to condemn them as monstrously inhuman is to conflate "the Orient" with our own recurring nightmare of the Occidental Other.

Which "image," then, captures the authentic Anna Leonowens? Is she a stubborn champion of human rights, or does this advocacy cloak a more ambiguous social role? By reading intertextually, that is, by analyzing the way in which *The King and I* cites, parodies, refutes, recuperates, and generally transforms *Uncle Tom's Cabin*, Margaret Landon's novel *Anna and the King of Siam*, and the diaries of Anna Leonowens, a feminist analysis can open up the contradictions between the film's stated discourse of liberation and the unstated discourse that controls its rhetorical systems. This reading also opens up our conception of gender, for it reveals that, both as constructed subject of her own narratives and as cinematic signifier, the character of "Anna" becomes a nodal point for a multiplicity of conflicting ideologies that make a univocal articulation of gender impossible. We can no longer determine Anna's gender one-dimensionally; instead, we must affirm "the incomplete, open and politically negotiable character of every identity."[36] Indeed, Anna could well be the prototype for de Lauretis's feminist revisioning of the social subject: "a subject constituted in gender, to be sure, though not by sexual difference alone, but rather across languages and cultural representations; a subject en-gendered in the experiencing of race and class, as well as sexual relations; a subject, therefore, not unified but rather multiple, and not so much divided as contradicted" (*TOG* 2).

But perhaps the narrator of Margaret Landon's *Anna and the*

King of Siam says it best when she observes that "without intent . . . [Anna] found herself set up between the oppressor and the oppressed." Instead of following Mira, who hides out in the women's room to escape the paradoxes of her life, white, middle-class feminism—like Mrs. Anna—must recognize and embrace these contradictions if it is to cultivate a position that does not undo itself from within. As the political writing on the wall (literally, the graffiti in French's "ladies' " room) suggests, we must have "a revolution of sensibility." Anything less will cost feminism its status as a truly inclusive and revolutionary movement for *all* women.

3

The Con of the Text

A world out of context allows an indeterminate number of solutions, and the listener is engaged in guessing what is meant.
Roman Jakobson, *"Language in Operation"*

A large rose-tree stood near the entrance of the garden: the roses growing on it were white, but there were three gardeners at it, busily painting them red. Alice thought this a very curious thing.
Lewis Carroll, Alice's Adventures in Wonderland

In their essay "Colonialism, Racism, and Representation: An Introduction," Robert Stam and Louise Spence issue a passionate call for an anticolonialist critical theory. Although they intend the filmic community as the particular audience for their plea, Stam and Spence's articulation of the issues—especially those pertaining to the relation of text and context—also speaks directly to the arena of contemporary feminism and the political/critical conundrums in which it is currently embroiled:

Although we are quite aware of the crucial importance of the *contextual*, that is . . . those social institutions and production practices which construct colonialism and racism in the cinema, our emphasis here will be *textual* and *intertextual*. An anti-colonialist analysis, in our view, must make the same kind of methodological leap effected by feminist criticism when . . . [it] critically transcended the usefully angry but methodologically flawed "image" [of women] analysis . . . in order to pose questions concerning the apparatus, the position of the spectator, and the specifically cinematic codes.[1]

According to Stam and Spence, a genuinely anticolonialist theory can emerge only if it sheds the "sensible" hermeneutic coat that context weaves from the fabric of referentiality and instead clothes itself with the much more haute-couture garb of textuality and intertextuality.

However, the feminist leap from the contextual to the textual or intertextual does not possess the unified momentum that Stam and Spence suggest, since many critics display an intense anxiety about the consequences of sacrificing their more traditional approach. For example, Elaine Showalter's critique of poststructuralism also exhibits a strong unease about the consequences of its turn away from a more historically and ethically based feminist analysis. The locus of her anxiety coheres in the special *Diacritics* issue devoted to feminism and deconstruction and especially in its cover portrait of the high-fashion textualist woman. According to Showalter, an elegantly dressed Diacritical covergirl sits in front of a white background "in a black tuxedo and high heels" sans head or hands. This portrait of a "woman" is completed on the back cover where "a dress, hat, gloves, and shoes arrange themselves in a graceful bodiless tableau in space. No 'vulgar' feminist, the chic Diacritical covergirl hints at the ephemera of gender identities or gender signatures."[2] The way this textualist image devalues the material specificity of women's lives (the invisibility and implied dismemberment of her body) and blurs "gender signatures" (its androgynous costuming) contributes to Showalter's fear that Diacritical covergirls (and boys) will violently uproot women from their historical and biological embeddedness. Like the gardeners of *Alice in Wonderland*, they paint the white roses red and deface political and social—not to mention horticultural—meaning. One should note that at least the gardeners in *Alice* painted the white roses red in order to rectify their mistake of planting white roses where the Queen of Hearts had ordered red ones. "And, if the Queen [of Hearts] was to find it out, we should all have our heads cut off, you know." For Showalter and other "traditional" feminists, the perceived vandalism of textuality can hardly claim such a pressing excuse.

Other feminist trajectories such as the allegedly flawed "images of women" approach articulated by Marcia Holly in her preface to the well-known anthology, *Patterns of Strength*, and "gynocriticism," Showalter's term for a cultural model of women's writing,[3] also refuse Stam and Spence's methodological leap. For "images of women" theorists, "literary criticism, like social science, can begin to be objective only when critics are informed about prevailing cultural myths, about the sexual, racial, and religious stereotypes that we as a people have internalized, and are therefore at the core of our hypotheses."[4] This position necessarily requires the dominance of context over text, since it mandates analysis of the content of women's lives within literature in order to determine the psychological authenticity or inauthenticity of these portrayals. In other words, feminist criticism must rely upon criteria external to the text, that is, reference to the "authentic" experience of actual women, for its hermeneutic principle of choice.

Because of its rootedness in cultural and social history, Showalter's "gynocriticism" foregrounds analysis similar to that of Clifford Geertz's "thick description" as one of its most important interpretive strategies: "Cultural anthropology and social history can perhaps offer us a terminology and a diagram of women's cultural situation. But feminist critics must use this concept in relation to what women actually write, not in relation to a theoretical, political, metaphoric, or visionary ideal of what women ought to write."[5] While not denying that these contextual approaches have produced extraordinarily valuable insights about the socialization and cultural position of women, it is important to note that they are also unfortunately predisposed to make essentialist generalizations about women's "authentic" experience—a tendency that literary historian Janet Todd identifies as the central weakness of "traditional" feminist criticism.

Although traditional feminism's story of women's writing is a unified "Aristotelian one with beginning, middle and end . . . this need not be so; instead it can be seen as episodic, serialized or multiple—there may be as many stories as one wants."[6] Deborah McDowell urges a similar caution toward the isolation of "thematic and imagistic commonalities" in African American women's literature when she argues that black feminist critics should beware of generalizing on the basis of too few examples.[7] It is ironic that in many instances, then, the contextual approach of traditional feminism seems only too little aware of history. Further, both "images of women" and "gynocritical" practitioners share the difficulties of other "theoreticians of reflection or homology"[8] who presume that texts transparently reproduce constitutive patterns of the socioeconomic structure. This positivist thematic emphasis leaves the structure of the text largely untouched and ignores the status of literary works "as complex and contradictory examples of materiality in their own right" with a textuality both linguistic and semiotic.[9]

I would argue that the subordination of context to text in the search for white or black "images of women," and of text to context in Stam and Spence's theoretical anticolonialism, is a "con," or a trick assumption, which in fact distorts the relationship of a literary work to its sociocultural production. By deconstructing the terms that have heretofore grounded the debate, however, both feminists and sympathetic critics such as Stam and Spence could forge an extremely powerful and subversive strategy of reading both contextually *and* textually, ideologically *and* semiotically. I will begin this task by reading the historical—one might say contextual—1905 memoirs of Mrs. Aeneas Gunn's year on a cattle station in the outback of Australia along with their cinematic portrayal in the 1982 Australian film, *We of the Never-Never* (also discussed in chapter 4). Through an examination of the triangle that develops among Mrs. Gunn, Bett-Bett (the young Aboriginal girl she adopts), and the men of the Elsey, I hope to formulate a model for articulating the relationship between text and context

The Con of the Text

55

that not only takes the historical particularity of women seriously but also raises questions about the text's signifying apparatus— the position of the viewer/reader and of specifically cinematic or literary codes.

Mrs. Aeneas Gunn's memoirs describe her struggles during the year (1902) that she spent as a bride and an intelligent, assertive white woman in the totally isolated male world of an Australian cattle station. When I first read them, I was also newly married and on the faculty at an all-white and all-male honors college that was forty-five miles and a steep mountain pass away from the nearest small town. As you can imagine, I felt a profound affinity for Mrs. Gunn that prompted the dialogic grafting of her very similar struggle for recognition in a masculinist community onto my own and the particularities of my experience onto hers. I borrow the trope of "grafting" from deconstruction because I believe that this particular metaphor suggestively poses the relationship between text and context and in so doing demonstrates the usefulness of certain poststructuralist constructs to anticolonialist and feminist criticism.

In his essay "The Double Session," Jacques Derrida explores the derivation of the terms "graph" and "graft" from the Greek root *graphion* (a writing implement or stylus) in order to posit an analogy between horticultural and textual grafting.[10] Horticultural grafting is a plant-propagating practice that roots one plant onto the body of another by either natural or artificial means. In such plants as climbing ivies, natural grafting occurs when sap passes from one ivy to another across a union of stems and then circulates within the second stem;[11] in artificial grafting, a union usually involves joining a scion, or the upper part of one plant, to a stock, or the rooted part of another, to form one plant. A horticulturalist usually employs this method for plants that are difficult to grow on their own root stems or for plants that cannot be grown easily from seeds, offsets, or cuttings.[12]

Textual graf(ph)ting simulates this practice, for like its botanical counterpart, writing infiltrates other texts and, according to Derrida, becomes "grafted onto the aborescence of another text." As such, graf(ph)ting explores the "structural nonsaturation" of context, that is, the ability of language "to function in new contexts with new force," and makes visible "the points of juncture and stress where one scion or line of argument has been spliced with another."[13] Graf(ph)ting as the combination of both these connotations could become an extraordinarily powerful trope for feminist criticism because it insists not only upon the text as a playful system of signs but also upon the material rootedness of signification. Signifiers, like flowers, cannot live without a vital connection to some "context"—whether it be sociohistorical reference or a rosebush. And nothing frames the usefulness of graf(ph)ting as a strategy of reading more dramatically than the opening scenes of the textual and intertextual re-presentation of Mrs. Gunn's "context" in the film, *We of the Never-Never*.

Shot number one, which unfolds even before the initial credits, reveals a mise-en-scène that focuses upon the close-up of a woman's face, radiant with an unknown anticipation. Shot number two quickly explains this anticipation by retreating to a full-length frontal view of the woman, whose name is "Jeannie" (Angela Punch McGregor), as she is being dressed by a maid for her wedding. A woman who we suspect is a relative takes over this chore, and another woman who appears to be Jeannie's mother solemnly imparts the following advice: never lose your femininity since you will have no female company in the wilds of the outback; do not try to be a "mate" to your husband since you are his wife and he will have his men for friends; grace his table and manage his servants since all men need these services from women. Jeannie responds to her mother's disquisition with the terse statement that she loves him and "that's all that matters."

An "images of women" approach to this scene might focus upon how the social institution of marriage, like the corset that the characters struggle to lace, binds Jeannie to an "inauthentic" social role within patriarchy; it might also examine how the women duplicate the practices of nineteenth-century domesticity or expose the ideology of romance embodied in Jeannie's emphatic segregation of love as the privileged criterion of judgment about male-female relationships. Gynocriticism, on the other hand, might excavate the cultural model of women's writing that Mrs. Gunn's autobiography represents. While I would not abandon the insights of these contextual feminist analyses, I would certainly extend them by considering what "sociocritic" Edmond Cros calls "the ideological semanticization of filmic [and literary] syntax and the medium itself":[14] in other words, how patriarchal and imperialist ideologies are graf(ph)ted onto the textual apparatus.

For example, the first scene of *We of the Never-Never* literally circumscribes the film's "women's room." Its physical embodiment exists as the inside of a drawing room, whose female inhabitants passively stand or sit. Through a panoramic and exhilarating scene of men—featuring the vastness of the outback (shot from an overhead helicopter) and the frenetic activity of cattle droving—the very next frame effectively seals the film's women in their claustrophobically gendered room. That women are also thematically segregated from the film's masculine world seems clear from the fact that its lone horseman is galloping to tell his incredulous "mates" that the "Boss" (Aeneas Gunn, played by Arthur Dignam) has "gotten himself married" and intends to bring to the cattle station that most exotic and despised of creatures—a woman. Further, unlike the women's room, whose inhabitants only speak unilaterally, this masculine scene allows us to glimpse these white and black men talking *to* each other, a phenomenon which falsely suggests that even Aboriginal men possess more prestige than white women.

The very sequence of these frames thus exposes a seam where the film splices patriarchal ideology into the textual apparatus of the film. At the very least, the effect of both content and signifying practice in these two scenes is to install the female characters firmly in the private domestic sphere of servants and household management and the male characters in the public sphere of action and paid work. Like its thematic counterpart, the filmic syntax in *We of the Never-Never* becomes a patriarchal discourse that constructs the feminine subject in/to sexual difference: defining women as dehumanized objects who, like fine china or sterling silver, grace their husbands' tables and segregating women and men through an ideology of separate spheres. From *We of the Never-Never*'s beginning moments, the relationship between text and context in the presentation of character sets a complicated mosaic of meaning into motion, for its visual representation of masculine and feminine experience graf(ph)ts a discourse of sexual difference not only onto the filmic characters but also onto the perspective of the spectators.

This pluralistic mediation of the text by viewers or readers is devalued by traditional feminist criticism's limited concept of context. In her introduction to *Reader-Response Criticism: From Formalism to Post-Structuralism*, Jane Tompkins notes that acknowledging the reader "constitutes the first step in a series that gradually breaks through the boundaries that separate the text from its producers and consumers and reconstitutes it as a web whose threads have no beginning and no end."[15] Graf(ph)ting re-articulates this insight through horticulturalist R. J. Garner's rationale for engaging in the delicate and risk-filled practice of plant splicing: "To enable one root system to support more than a single variety or one branch system to derive from more than one root system" (*GH* 35). According to Garner, "In [grafting] thoroughly compatible unions, where the fibres are firmly interlocked, there is no free passage for all materials or intermixing of tissues. Each component retains its own special characteristics right up to the junction" (*GH* 59). As a trope for the relation between spectator or reader and text, graf(ph)ting both affirms the insertion of multiple perspectives into the viewing/reading experience and preserves the material particularity of each interpreter. The reader neither absorbs the text in an unchecked free passage of hermeneutic activity, nor does her interpretive activity become intermixed with some univocal textual meaning. This emphasis on graf(ph)ting as a process of both the reader/spectator and the text questions the traditional definition of context as an objective, monolithic entity by demonstrating the protean and fluid nature of any contextual boundaries. The nonlinearity of the web connecting text and reader contravenes the extremes both of a feminist criticism that locates meaning in some extratextual social reference and of poststructuralisms that locate it only within the text itself.

However, I want to expand this discussion of graf(ph)ting even further by invoking an overlooked, yet equally important, etymological connotation: graft as political corruption. This meaning of "graft" originated in the Teapot Dome scandal of the Harding administration: the horticultural practice clearly described how such

men as Doheny and Fall amassed substantial private fortunes—
and political power—by "grafting" illegal practices onto their
legal offices. Graf(ph)ting as the acquisition and maintenance of
power refocuses the relation of text and context by foregrounding
the question of ideology, or the discursive intersection of belief systems and political power.[16] Although theorists and activists have
defined ideology in many different ways, most of these definitions
share the following common elements: "A dominant power may
legitimate itself by *promoting* beliefs and values congenial to it;
naturalizing and *universalizing* such beliefs so as to render them
self-evident and apparently inevitable; *denigrating* ideas which
might challenge it; *excluding* rival forms of thought, perhaps by
some unspoken but systematic logic; and *obscuring* social reality
in ways convenient to itself."[17] The process of graf(ph)ting not
only undergirds these strategies but also emphasizes ideology as
the production of "conflicts within the field of signification."[18]
In *We of the Never-Never*, the development of the relationship
between Mrs. Gunn and Bett-Bett dramatically shows how the
latter sense of ideology might work within a text and convincingly
demonstrates its necessity to any anticolonialist feminist theory.

We of the Never-Never first presents "Bett-Bett," the young Aboriginal girl whom Mrs. Gunn adopts, during the scene where
Mr. Gunn introduces his wife to her domestic staff. This scene is
particularly interesting for its contextual similarity to the film's
shot of the Elsey's whitemale drovers rounding up their livestock:
both "lubras" and cattle are herded to the homestead and both are
situated only in nondistinct generic groups. Since Bett-Bett is a part
of the domestic staff's group, she is initially placed in a nonhuman
position vis-à-vis the film's white characters. The textual codes of
cinematographic image scale and duration, which are intricately
related to the respect afforded a character (CRR 644), reinforce
this contextual subordination, for the duration of Mrs. Gunn's
facial close-up lasts a full three seconds longer than that of Bett-
Bett. Here, both context and text work hand in hand to uncover a
similar meaning effect: the colonization of the character Bett-Bett
through *We of the Never-Never*'s signifying practices.

In *The Role of the Reader: An Exploration in the Semiotics of
Texts*, Umberto Eco notes that the reader actualizes the meaning of

the text by singling out its elementary ideological structures. This operation is overdetermined by the reader/spectator's own ideological subcodes: "This means that not only the outline of textual ideological structures is governed by the ideological bias of the reader but also that a given ideological background can help one to discover or to ignore textual ideological structures." [19] Thus, while Anglo-European women watching the film might single out the exclusion and ridicule that Mrs. Gunn receives at the hands of the Elsey's men as its elementary ideological structure, women (or men) of color might feel angry or oppressed at its imperialist discourse of white=human, Aboriginal=nonhuman. After all, the nineteenth-century cattle station closely parallels the southern plantation in that white women were more often the oppressors rather than the sisters of black women. The material specificity of graf(ph)ting as a trope for reading helps counteract the essentialist Reader/Spectator who inhabits much current "reader-response theory" and feminist criticism's elaboration of the Woman Reader. Graf(ph)ting questions such universalism because it requires a complex negotiation of text and contexts—both of the text's cultural production and the ideological embeddedness of the reader/spectator.

A concrete example is *We of the Never-Never*'s highlighting of Mrs. Gunn's resistance to her marginalization and her eventual prevalence over the Elsey's men and its denial of this to Bett-Bett and the other Aboriginal women of the cattle station. If we read *We of the Never-Never* intertextually—that is, as a splicing of Mrs. Gunn's memoirs into the filmic narrative—a disparity emerges that throws the character of Bett-Bett into disturbing relief. The film actually combines two published works of Mrs. Gunn—*We of the Never-Never* and *The Little Black Princess* (1905)—the latter focusing primarily on the story of Bett-Bett. Mrs. Gunn's diaries portray Bett-Bett as an indomitable, irrepressible, courageous, and resourceful girl. Indeed, *The Little Black Princess* begins with Bett-Bett's thrilling encounter with another group of Aborigines who attack the members of her tribe; she escapes by swimming to a steep bank, standing underwater on an old tree root, and remaining motionless for hours until the threat of danger passed. This spirit completely disappears in the filmic graf(ph)ting of Bett-Bett's character. However, the starkest contrast of the character in *The Little Black Princess* to the timid, passive, and silent young girl of the film occurs in the book's description of Bett-Bett's behavior during a fight between her puppy Sue and the other dogs of the cattle station: "With a shriek, Bett-Bett flew to the rescue. As she ran, she picked up a thick stick, and with it fought and hammered and screamed her way into the biting, yelping mob of dogs; then, picking up the dusty little speckled ball, she fought and hammered and screamed her way out again to a place of safety."[20]

We of the Never-Never's negative graf(ph)ting of Bett-Bett becomes even more surprising when we consider the film's explicitly feminist overtones: through the voices of the men, it tries to illuminate the psychosocial supports for sexism, and through the voice of Mrs. Gunn, to present a case against the position of women as second-class citizens. However, I would argue that, although the film does make some attempt to link Anglo-European attitudes toward women with imperialist attitudes toward aboriginal peoples, the presentation of Bett-Bett's character makes the case against sexism at the expense of a stance against racism. Even more disturbingly, the film uses its antisexist rhetoric to displace questions of colonialism, racism, and their concomitant violence.

A good example of such semiotic and ideological graf(ph)t occurs in the scene immediately following the film's introduction of Bett-Bett. In this scene, Mrs. Gunn asks Bett-Bett if she would like some "tucker," or food, to which Bett-Bett docilely responds in the affirmative. They walk over to the kitchen (a building separate from the homestead), and Mrs. Gunn asks Sam Lee, the Chinese cook, whether she can scramble some eggs for herself and her charge. Sam Lee refuses by insisting that he is the cook, so Mrs. Gunn asks him to cook them breakfast. A thoroughly unpleasant fellow, Sam Lee barks out that he "cook for men, cook for Missy," but—looking directly at Bett-Bett—"no cook for damn black." Most viewers recoil from this aggressive expression of bigotry and applaud when, in a voice shaking with moral righteousness, Mrs. Gunn defends Bett-Bett with an ultimatum that either he or she will scramble those eggs. She wins and Sam Lee cooks—both for her and the "damn black" he so despises.

Beyond its reinforcement of the passive Bett-Bett as needing the maternalistic protection of white women and the active Mrs. Gunn as virtuously providing it, this scene also ingeniously mystifies the systemic oppression of white supremacy by focusing on the localized individual prejudice of the itinerant worker Sam Lee. The above exchange leaves no doubt in the viewer's mind about his individual bias; what it obscures, however, is the fact that a dispossessed laborer historically possessed neither the means nor the power for any individual prejudice to have far-reaching results. The real question is why a seemingly "progressive" film constructs a political scene where a member of the oppressing group—Mrs. Gunn—confronts the oppressed—Sam Lee—concerning his bigotry yet fails to confront the issue of the brutal physical and epistemic violence that the white population used to gain control of Aboriginal lands for cattle stations such as the Elsey.

This also begs the question of *We of the Never-Never*'s critique of violence against women. The instructive sequence here is the encounter between whites and blacks on the Elsey after Mrs. Gunn's female domestic staff disappears, forcing her to finish the cleaning alone. Jack, the "boss" in charge of the Elsey's provisions, reminds the Aboriginal group that their white masters gave them flour and tobacco but unless they worked, they would receive no rations at all. As Richard Broome remarks in *Aboriginal Australians: Black Response to White Dominance, 1788–1980*, whites and blacks on cattle stations coexisted through a precarious interdependence, but no phenomenon marked the subordinated position of blacks within this relationship more dramatically than the food they were given to eat: it not only signified their powerlessness, but the poor quality of the diet no doubt accounted for much of the lethargy of Mrs. Gunn's "lubras."[21]

During Jack's speech, Mrs. Gunn hears a commotion and looks over to see an Aborigine named Charlie beginning to beat Julie, his wife and one of Mrs. Gunn's errant domestic workers. She strides over to the quarreling group and demands that Charlie stop beating Julie. Her meddling in Aboriginal affairs is not taken well either by the group's men or by the women, and Mr. Gunn wisely (and paternalistically) explains to her that "we must accept their way of living." Like the previous encounter with Sam Lee, the cumulative effect of this scene graf(ph)ts a link between the "primitive" character of the male Aborigine and violence against women by implying that it exists as a natural part of their tribal life. But perhaps, one might think, the men's very powerlessness leads them to assert their own power over women. To catch the bitter irony of this particular implication, however, we need to return to the film's opening masculine scene.

As described earlier, this scene focuses upon the galloping horseman rushing to tell his mates of Gunn's intent to bring his wife to the outback. Jack relays this information to Billy Muck, one of the Aboriginal drovers, in the midst of their calf roping. "Good," Billy replies, partly in earnest, partly in jest. "Maybe now they'll leave our women alone." Billy Muck's remark is literally relegated to the margins of the film, both textually and contextually. In spite of this marginalization, however, it quietly works to re-place *We of the Never-Never*'s displacement of violence against women. To this end, Richard Broome observes that

> Aboriginal women probably suffered the worst abuse at the hands of their European bosses. Sexual oppression has always gone hand in hand with conquest and exploitation and it was perhaps inevitable on the north Australian frontier where the rough-and-tumble European adventurers came without their own women. . . . Male chauvinism and racism underpinned the attitudes of most European men in the Territory. . . . Many whites claimed that they were lured to the north by adventure, money and Aboriginal women. The old Territory joke was that Europeans were "sexplorers" who sought the joys of "black velvet." [22]

Instances of violence against women were certainly recorded within Aboriginal groups. Again, however, the textual apparatus of *We of the Never-Never* mystifies racist and sexist oppression by displacing it down the chain of signifiers from their appropriate sources and onto their historical victims. Such a process confirms the suspicion of "sociocriticism" that elements in the text related to a specific ideological discourse no longer refer the reader to a set of abstract principles constituting that discourse but rather reproduce this relation in terms of its "metonymical virtualities." [23] This certainly qualifies as the cinematic equivalent of *Alice*'s gardeners painting the white roses red.

This discussion of graf(ph)ting in *We of the Never-Never* has, I hope, persuasively illustrated that we cannot consider questions raised by the play of signifiers without simultaneously examining their context, or, according to Stam and Spence, "those social institutions and production practices which construct colonialism and racism in the cinema." However, the reverse is also true: one cannot consider the social institutions and production practices that construct colonialism and racism without exploring their dissemination and mediation within the play of a particular text. Rather than the antagonistic bond of matter (context) and antimatter (text), the relationship of text and context becomes a non-disjunctive one that, according to Richard Terdiman in *Discourse/Counter-Discourse: The Theory and Practice of Symbolic Resistance in Nineteenth-Century France*, requires that we specify the complex modes of translation and transformation between them.[24]

Just as the context of *We of the Never-Never* reveals the "con" of its text, that is, the trick assumptions of an allegedly antisexist film that in fact absolve Anglo-European men and women of their responsibility for colonialist violence, graf(ph)ting reveals the "con" of the alleged opposition between text and context. Thus, it bequeaths feminism a strategy not only for reading both historical and fictional experience but also for interrogating the way in which this experience becomes a victim of, or complicit with, the political corruption of graft. In themselves, text and context are inadequate as antipatriarchal and anticolonialist weapons; together, they metamorphose into a relentlessly subversive strategy of reading. Indeed, without an adequate appropriation of graf(ph)ting's materialist semiotics, feminist criticism is in danger of creating its own Teapot Dome scandal, which will inevitably come crashing down upon its theoretical head.

The Problem of Discourse in a
Marxist Never-Never Land

4

Of "Piccaninnies"
and Peter Pan

ON FALSE DICHOTOMIES

Is there no way out except submission to the heart of the colonial
community or departure? Yes, still one. . . . Why not knock at the
door of the colonized whom he defends and who would surely open
their arms to him in gratitude? He has discovered that one of the
camps is that of injustice, the other, then, is that of righteousness.
Let him take one more step, let him complete his revolt to the full.
The colony is not made up only of Europeans! Refusing the colonizers, damned by them: let him adopt the colonized people and be
adopted by them; let him become a turncoat.

    Albert Memmi, *The Colonizer and the Colonized*

If it wishes to survive as a revolutionary movement, Euro-Ameri-
can feminism must ask the question posed by Albert Memmi: Are
there no alternatives to colonialism except presence or absence?
According to Memmi, one could intervene in this false dichotomy

with a third position: that of "adoption" by the colonized. However, a colonizer who merely sympathizes with the plight of the
colonized falls short of this position; the colonizer must also be
loved by the colonized.[1] Memmi's insistence on the colonizer's
existential, and not just intellectual, participation in the life of the
oppressed also captures Gayatri Spivak's meaning when she describes how Anglo-European feminists usually "wander out of our
own academic and First-World enclosure": "When we speak for
ourselves, we urge with conviction: the personal is also the political. For the rest of the world's women, the sense of whose personal
micrology is difficult (though not impossible) for us to acquire,
we fall back on a colonialist theory of most efficient information
retrieval."[2] Information retrieval can never liberate one from the
position of the colonizer because the "Third World" woman still
remains the "object" of information and the "First World" feminist the distanced and superior interpreter of that information.

If we look for female members of colonizing groups who have
renounced their positions and become adopted by the colonized,
the unforgettable image of Daisy Bates (1861–1951), "the Great
White Queen of the Never-Never," comes vividly to mind. Bates,
who left a journalistic career in England to live in the northern
Australian desert wilderness with the Ngalli-a, the Arunta, the
Wong-gai-i-Waddi, and the Koogurda, began her life's vocation
with an offer in 1899 to investigate exploitation of Aboriginal cultures by white settlers. Douglas Glass's famous photograph of her
frames a formidable woman seated on a porch, with an umbrella
firmly clasped in one white-gloved hand and a large leather purse
clutched in the other, her high-top boots neatly laced, and a crisply
starched high-necked collar highlighting the stubborn jut of her
jaw. In his foreword to Bates's memoirs, Alan Moorehead muses
upon this remarkable photograph: "A glance at the photograph
and one feels one knows her pretty well—the eccentric, voyaging,
Victorian spinster, pert and indestructible, the missionary figure:
Florence Nightingale or perhaps the lady who went off to the court
of the King of Siam. She is one's well-loved maiden aunt."[3] If the
journeys of Bates's life share some particulars with those of her
historical sister, Mrs. Anna Leonowens, then they also share some
of the contradictions.

Of "Piccaninnies" and Peter Pan

On one level, Daisy Bates seems to exemplify Memmi's portrait of the colonizer who "refuses," for she quickly passed beyond the task of retrieving information about the Aborigines and became an adopted member of their tribe: "They accepted me as a kindred spirit. . . . They even allowed me free access to the sacred places and the sacred ceremonies of the initiations of the men, which their own women must never see under penalty of death."[4] Further, according to Bates, "at the men's hidden corroborees, far from my own people in the heart of the bush, because I showed no quiver of timidity, or of revulsion of feeling, or of levity, because I was thinking with my 'black man's mind,' I have never been a stranger" (PA 25). "Thinking black" was Daisy Bates's articulation of identification with the oppressed, and no one could deny that they greatly loved her. After all, what other white person voluntarily lived for years in a fourteen-foot circular tent in extremes of heat, wind, and cold for the sole purpose of ameliorating the disruptions of colonization by tending and comforting its aboriginal victims?

While Bates remained highly skeptical of women's emancipation and the appearance of the New Woman in Britain (once denouncing such women as "Public Nuisances"), she nevertheless became an ardent advocate for Aboriginal women. Kabbarli, or "grandmother," as Bates was called, particularly resisted their exchange as commodified objects and mounted a vigorous campaign to rectify the situation: "There were four Manilamen at Beagle Bay married to native women. By tribal custom the women had all been betrothed in infancy to their rightful tribal husbands. They were therefore merely on hire by their own men to the Asiatics, and, in spite of the church marriage, remained, not only their husband's property, but that of all his brothers, and all of the Manila husband's brothers who paid for the accommodation. It was hard to convince the Bishop and the little abbot of this fact and of the terrible cruelty to the women and girls of such a system" (PA 12). Her outrage at the exploitation of these women knew no racial bounds, and she criticized both Anglo and Aboriginal men for perpetuating this oppressive and brutal misogynist network.

However, despite an adoption by the colonized that transgressed virtually every British social more, Bates simultaneously embodied the difficulties of refusal. Memmi persuasively argues in *The Colonizer and the Colonized* that privilege lies at the heart of the colonial relationship. Indeed, he asks, what is colonialism "if not a regime of oppression for the benefit of a few? The entire administrative and political machinery of a colony has no other goal. The human relationships have arisen from the severest exploitation, founded on inequality and contempt, guaranteed by police authoritarianism" (CC 62). In her own relationships with Aboriginal peoples, Daisy Bates seemed to jettison the flotsam of colonialism, for her severely nomadic life exhibited few of the qualities that one might describe as "privileged." However, colonial privilege is not solely economic (CC xii)—or, for Daisy Bates, related to the refusal of middle-class living arrangements.

As the analysis of Mrs. Anna Leonowens has shown, empires exist through complex relationships of control, and we can disregard no strategy or micrology of power that disseminates them. Paternalism is one such strategy. This "astonishing mental attitude" stretches racism and inequality to its tautest logical extremes: "It is, if you like, a charitable racism—which is not thereby less skillful nor less profitable. . . . Having found this new moral order where he is by definition master and innocent, the colonialist would at last have given himself absolution" (CC 760). In spite of her profound concern for the "dying" Aborigines and her protestation of the paternalistic "kindness that killed as surely and as swiftly as cruelty would have done," Daisy Bates acts as what one might call a colonial maternalist because she ensnares the very groups she protects with discourses of control.

Like a mother tending her children, Bates found it impossible "to leave these people, to be deaf to their appeal for human kindliness, and of the hopelessness of any movement except one of help and personal example. So savage and so simple, so much astray and so utterly helpless were they, that somehow they became my responsibility" (PA 207). This perception of Aboriginal society as infantile functioned as the basis for the colonialist discourse of the "piccaninny"—one of the most powerful justifications of Anglo-European imperialism and the subject of this chapter. However, it is the memoirs of Mrs. Aeneas Gunn, another great white queen of the Never-Never, that most tellingly expose the disparity between action and speech in the crucible of colonialism. Precisely *because* of their contradictory social positioning, the differences within themselves, the women of colonial Australia illuminate some of the most complex historical and theoretical issues of the imperialist project.

WILL MARXISM EVER GROW UP?; OR, HOW NEVER-NEVER LAND RE-VISIONS REVOLUTION

Marxism is a revolutionary world outlook which must always strive for new discoveries, which completely despises rigidity in once-valid theses, and whose living force is best preserved in the intellectual clash of self-criticism and the rough and tumble of history.

Rosa Luxemburg, *The Anti-Critique*

"1701: Sao Salvador de Bahia, *Voice of America*: Father António Vieira died at the turn of the century, but not so his voice. . . . The words of this missionary to the poor and persecuted still echo with the same lively ring throughout the lands of Brazil." [5] Father António Vieira—or more precisely, Father Vieira's voice—articulates a question from beyond the grave that continues to haunt Marxist analysis: How can such an intimate effect of the body survive the body itself? Of course, the passage implies that what survives is not his physiological voice but rather a mode of communication, a discourse, that resonates independently of its actual speaker. Following Emile Benveniste, we could label "discourse" any enunciation "distinguished . . . by its integration of both the locutor and the listener with the desire of the former to influence the latter." [6] This definition does not quite account for Father Vieira's spectral echo, however, since in this instance the desire to influence listeners survives his mortal ability to converse.

In *The History of Sexuality*, Michel Foucault extends the problem of Father Vieira's "voice," or discourse, beyond the sphere of the individual in his assertion that discourses constitute tactical blocks which operate in the field of force relations and which "we must question on the two levels of their productivity (what reciprocal effects of power and knowledge they ensure) and their strategical integration (what conjunction and what force relationship make their utilization necessary in a given episode of the various confrontations that occur)."[7] It is precisely this involvement in the production and transmission of power that makes the interpretation of discourse so indispensable for Marxist analysis— particularly for its analysis of colonialism.

An example that illustrates the importance of discursive processes to the success of the colonialist project emerges in the link that the discourse of the Catholic church forged between the economic exploitation of indigenous South American groups and the subordination of women. In her research on the historical role of the church in the colonization of the Americas, anthropologist Eleanor Leacock documents the efforts of orders such as the Jesuits to impose a model of the patriarchal nuclear family, complete with Europeanized norms of sexual and conjugal behavior, upon such tribes as the Montagnais-Maskape:

> The Jesuit attack on the autonomy of women was compounded by a systematic attack on individual autonomy specifically and egalitarian relations in general. Control of a husband and father over a wife and offspring, along with control of men over other men, were seen by the Jesuits as the key to restructuring productive relations and attitudes toward colonial domination, bringing the Indians from "savagery" to "civilization." The Jesuit program of conversion had devastating effects on zealots and their victims, fomenting internal conflict and creating the divide-and-rule situation that is the ever present tool of colonization.[8]

The theological discourses of Catholicism exacerbated inequalities and effectively undermined those social, political, and economic institutions that guaranteed women's rights and, by extension, the rights of indigenous peoples.[9]

Marx himself suggests the centrality of such discourses to any analysis of colonialism in his sweeping reference to the "Christian colonial system" and his directive that "this stuff ought to be studied in detail, to see what the bourgeois makes of himself and of the worker when he can model the world according to his own image without any interference."[10] A bourgeois remodeling of the world with no interference from resisting forces could easily describe the ideological core of the discursive process and, at the very least, implies an intersection of language and power that demands further investigation. In spite of these provocative allusions, however, discourse's life on the margins of historical materialism—literally, confined to a footnote of *Capital*—has limited Marxism's ability to explain the semiotic means by which groups maintain their power. Perhaps the most important message of Father Vieira's voice, then, is the inadequacy of Marxism's traditional base-superstructure paradigm for considering these cultural phenomena, since it elucidates neither how discourses are formed nor the roles they play within social formations.[11]

I will attempt to explore the relationship of discourse and its social grounding by reading it through the lens of two turn-of-the-century texts: James M. Barrie's classic children's tale *Peter Pan* (originally *Peter and Wendy*, 1911) and *We of the Never-Never* (1905), Mrs. Aeneas Gunn's autobiographical account of the year that she spent on a cattle station in the northern outback of Australia. At this point, one might legitimately ask about the appropriateness of using literary works as vehicles for reformulating Marxist analysis. I would answer such questions by appealing to Antonio Gramsci's insight that narrative provides "a means of ideological diffusion which has a rapidity, a field of action, and an emotional simultaneity" which makes it an extremely potent yet contradictory instrument:[12] it exists not only as a weapon in disseminating ideology but also as a tool for unraveling the very disseminations it weaves.

Both *Peter Pan* and *We of the Never-Never* are deeply embedded in the historical context of British imperialism, and both possess fields of narrative action that reveal how discourses not only empower but also perpetuate this colonialist project. For example, through its reliance upon the enthymeme, or the rhetorical construction of an incomplete syllogism, *Peter Pan* dramatizes the importance of "articulating practices" to a hegemonic group, while *We of the Never-Never* indicates that discourses assume an "anaclitic" (literally, a "leaning-up-against") relationship with their material bases. I hope to demonstrate that discourses occupy a position which resists not only those "vulgar" Marxist interpretations that regard them merely as reflections of an economic base but also those which believe that discourses, like Never-Never Land, are only "make-believe" constructs of the bourgeois imagination.

"Second to the right, and straight on 'til morning." Everyone—that is, every Anglo-European child whose parents lulled him or her to sleep with bedtime stories—knows that these are the directions to Never-Never Land in *Peter Pan*, James M. Barrie's delightfully wicked tale of juvenile mayhem and adventure.[13] I myself dreamed longingly of waking like Wendy in the middle of the night and discovering Peter crying softly for his lost shadow. In gratitude for sewing his shadow back on, he would sprinkle me with fairy dust and I would fly to his magic island, fight Captain Hook, and become a mother to the Lost Boys. But much to my childish dismay, I learned that, like Santa Claus, Peter Pan's Never-Never Land was only "make-believe"; or, in more adult terms, it "relinquished any ostensive function, i.e., any connection with the 'here' and 'now' of reality, and therefore, any claim to 'truth value.'"[14] (Perhaps this insight conjures in different terms Peter's passionate desire always to be a boy and have fun.)

In *Marxism and Philosophy*, Alex Callinicos notes the limitations of this view for a Marxist, and indeed any other kind of politically committed, analysis:

A Truth-conditional theory of meaning gives a formal and structural account of language. . . . Such an account may be valid as an explanation of how expressions are assigned their sense and reference and can probably be extended to deal with the force with which utterances are taken (as commands, assertions, etc.). It is, however, only an imperfect guide to the study of linguistic usage, and of its imbrication in social practice. . . . The reason is that formal semanticists, like analytical philosophers generally, are concerned with the *logical form* of expressions. . . . Now logic is concerned with valid inference; it appraises arguments in terms of their structure, sentences related in a particular inference. Entirely justifiably, it is not concerned with the question of whether or not there are relations between sentences other than those which transmit truth or falsity.[15]

By displaying a propensity toward "make-believe so real . . . that during a meal of it you could see him getting rounder" (*PP* 66), Peter Pan himself exists as a more reliable guide to these "other" relations that imbricate language within social practice. Peter's expanding girth whimsically emphasizes not only the text as discourse, or a communicative interaction of implied speakers, consciousnesses, and communities,[16] but also its materialist character. For Barrie's text, worldliness is not like some thief in the night who breaks into and out of textuality (or windows of the Darlings' house) at will, for the discursive effect of the meal (that we see him getting rounder) replaces the meal itself as the consuming— and consumed—interpretive matter.

However, the Lost Boys complain loudly about the coerciveness of Peter's particular propensity, since "if they broke down in their make-believe he [Peter] rapped them on the knuckles" (*PP* 59). The painful experience of the Lost Boys in Never-Never Land highlights the more somber fact that discourses and their various effects do not exist solely in the realm of consciousness, or, in Marxist terminology, in the superstructure. Indeed, the Lost Boys beg the question of articulating practices for a Marxist analysis, a question that emerges most urgently in the search for *Peter Pan*'s lost girl—the "belle of the Piccaninnies," Tiger Lily.

I conceived my own passion for *Peter Pan* during its revival as a Leonard Bernstein musical in the 1950s. One of my most vivid memories from this play was the duet sung by Peter and Tiger Lily celebrating Peter's heroic rescue of the Indian princess from the evil machinations of Captain Hook. Its chorus repeatedly professed undying mutuality and regard; however, if we examine the sociopolitical actualities of Barrie's text, a much different dynamic emerges:

> On the trail of the pirates, stealing noiselessly down the war-path, which is not visible to inexperienced eyes, come the redskins, every one of them with his eyes peeled. They carry tomahawks and knives, and their naked bodies gleam with paint and oil. Strung around them are scalps, of boys as well as of pirates, for these are the Piccaninny tribe. . . . Bringing up the rear, the place of greatest danger, comes Tiger Lily,

proudly erect, a princess in her own right. She is the most beautiful of dusky Dianas and the belle of the Piccaninnies, coquettish, cold and amorous by turns; there is not a brave who would not have the wayward thing to wife, but she staves off the altar with a hatchet. (*PP* 46)

At first glance, Tiger Lily seems literally to embody her name: "Tiger" evoking fierceness and amazonian stature, and "Lily," beauty and whiteness. Since Never-Never Land had never never allowed women to immigrate there as "real" citizens, Tiger Lily also appears as a welcome antidote to the staunchly conservative maternalism of Wendy (Peter: "What we need is just a nice motherly person." "Oh dear!" Wendy said, "You see I feel that is exactly what I am"). Although Peter explains that the absence of female inhabitants is merely because girls are too clever to fall out of their prams, one could just as easily conjecture that it is because women and women's traditional domestic labors are not highly thought of on Peter's island—an attitude (melo)dramatized by the fate of Starkey the pirate. During the final rout of Captain Hook and his crew by Peter and the Lost Boys, Starkey flees by swimming ashore. He is captured by the redskins, who, by way of punishment, "made him nurse for all their papooses, a melancholy come-down for a pirate" (*PP* 135). Against this misogyny, Tiger Lily inscribes a subversive female presence by refusing either to become the surrogate mother or to surrender her independence to Edwardian wifehood.

Yet something peculiar happens when we examine Barrie's portrayal of Tiger Lily as the belle of the Piccaninnies, for "piccaninny"—the West Indian derivative of *pequeño*—connotes "tiny," or "very little," and was commonly applied to black indigenous populations by their Anglo-European colonizers. Marlon Riggs's important documentary *Ethnic Notions* highlights the influence of the "piccaninny" as one of the most important images shaping Western attitudes about race.[17] For example, it shows a relief carved for the 1915 entrance gate of the San Francisco Exposition that metamorphoses a small black child into a "piccaninny" by making its braids stick out with a preternatural energy, emphasizing its wide toothless grin and imbuing its face with a decidedly demonic expression. Even more revealing are early cartoons included in the documentary that often portrayed "piccaninnies" as partially naked, dirty, and unkempt victims of nonhuman predators such as alligators or wolves—a scenario whose subhuman savagery betrays a deep racial ambivalence about the participation of African Americans in Anglo-European society. Indeed, this image of the "piccaninny" implies that only white law and morality can contain black lawlessness and amorality, and one could argue that its message not only reflects but also creates the rationale for maintaining white racial hegemony. As the narrator observes, "these caricatures did as much harm as any lynch mob" to African Americans, and the fact that they inflicted their wounds indirectly only meant that they were far more difficult to heal.

The question then becomes how *Peter Pan* yokes the apparent oxymoron of the full-sized white adult and the small black "piccaninny" in the character of Tiger Lily with such seeming ease and noncontradiction. To understand this phenomenon, we need to delve into the discipline of classical rhetoric and its practice of the incomplete syllogism or "enthymeme." Although Aristotle identified the enthymeme as a form of public reasoning used only by ignorant men, later Roman and medieval rhetoric defined it somewhat more kindly in terms of its elliptical argument, or the suppression of one or more relevant propositions.[18] Aristotle's *Rhetoric* captures this ellipticism when it states that "the Enthymeme must consist of a few propositions, fewer often than those which make up the normal syllogism. For if any of these propositions is a familiar fact, there is no need even to mention it; the hearer adds it himself" (1.2). The way an enthymeme both depends upon and solicits the suppressed premise surfaces in a contemporary version of it: the often heard accusation "since you are not pro-life [on the question of abortion], you are not a Christian":

(Suppressed) Premise I: All Christians must be pro-life.
Premise II: You are not pro-life.
Conclusion: You are not a Christian.

This succinct constellation of statements is an enthymeme because its major premise—that all Christians must be pro-life—is suppressed. To those "pro-lifers" articulating the syllogism, the hidden proposition seems an incontestable one that they simply keep in mind, or *en thumo*, as classical rhetoricians would say.[19] However, this suppression *en thumo* illustrates perhaps the primary ideological manipulation performed by enthymemes: based on a previous bias (here, a certain politics of Christianity), it chooses a given circumstantial selection that attributes a certain property to a sememe ("pro-life") and thereby conceals other contradictory properties that are equally predicable.[20] Of course, the equally predicable conclusion that our pro-life enthymeme suppresses is that one can be a Christian and favor a pro-choice position on abortion. By an enthymemic sleight of hand, however, one can superimpose the marker "pro-life" with its conservative political code onto the marker "Christian" with its diverse religious codes and reach a "foregone," albeit unsound, conclusion. In the case of abortion, the pro-life motivation for suppressing the crucial premise seems overwhelmingly clear: if God is on your side, you possess a potent argument indeed.

Although the text of *Peter Pan* imbues Tiger Lily with the possibility of challenging dominant interpretations of gender in fin-de-siècle imperial England, it also takes away this possibility by recuperating her within an implied enthymeme of the "Piccaninny"—that colonialist and paternalistic marker of a childish and less developed, therefore unequal, person. As Michèle Barrett remarks in *Women's Oppression Today: Problems in Marxist Feminist Analysis*, " 'Recuperation' . . . [is] the ideological effort that goes into negating and defusing challenges to the historically dominant meaning of gender in particular periods"—it takes away with one hand what you have given with the other.[21] *Peter Pan* accomplishes this process by constructing the following enthymeme:

> Premise I: Tiger Lily is a woman.
> (Suppressed) Premise II: Women and Piccaninnies are coextensive.
> Conclusion: Tiger Lily is belle of the Piccaninnies.

Like the above pro-life syllogism, this one also suppresses its critical premise that women have become coextensive with the "piccaninny" or "native" Other. This suppression successfully recuperates Tiger Lily's implicitly feminist challenge to traditional roles for women by subsuming her under the racist discourses of Anglo-European colonialism.

Peter Pan's use of the enthymeme clearly demonstrates the function and importance of a dominant group's "articulatory practices" to a radical political analysis. In *Hegemony and Socialist Strategy: Towards a Radical Democratic Politics*, Ernesto Laclau and Chantal Mouffe's provocative re-visioning of Marxism, articulatory practices establish "a relation among elements such that their identity is modified as a result." [22] In other words, just as a "practice" transforms material through time, a written practice (such as the enthymeme) exerts a continuously transformative effect upon the signifying material of language. [23] Articulatory practices work by constructing "nodal points," or privileged points that partially fix the meaning of a discursive chain; rather than expressing a previously self-defined totality (a deterministic base-superstructure argument), however, they create new positions of difference and invest any stable system of differences such as class, race, or sex with an incomplete "floating" character. [24] For Laclau and Mouffe, framing hegemony in the terms of articulatory practice redresses the spectacular failure of Marxism's base-superstructure model to detect how dominant groups such as the church or ruling classes constantly reinscribe their interests within society and successfully reorganize the result of this struggle. [25]

In *Peter Pan*, Tiger Lily's enthymeme becomes an articulatory practice when it creates new positions of difference by establishing a relation (syllogistic) among elements (woman and "piccaninny") that consequently modifies their identities (each becomes assimilated to the other). Since biographical testimony reveals that James M. Barrie "never talked politics himself," [26] one cannot assume that this ideological transformation is intentional on the part of the author; yet, this particular inscription of difference becomes politically crucial to the continued success of English colonial ambitions. It also greatly enlarges the field of categories that a Marxist analysis can use to account for imperialist social relations. [27] As Laclau and Mouffe note, such articulatory practices as synonymy, metonymy, metaphor—and I would add, the enthymeme—"are not forms of thought that add a second sense to a primary, constitutive literality of social relations; instead, they are part of the primary terrain itself in which the social is constituted."[28]

If articulatory practices "pierce the entire material density" of the multiplicitous institutions and rituals through which a discursive formation becomes structured,[29] then *Peter Pan*'s practice of the enthymeme constitutes a part of the primary social terrain that structures colonialist discourses. For example, the recuperation of Tiger Lily to the status of colonized object uncovers one of the most important sociocultural processes that enabled England to become the empire upon which the sun never set—a process that unfolds most revealingly in *Peter Pan*'s description of Peter and Tiger Lily's ultimate fate:

> Peter had saved Tiger Lily from a dreadful fate, and now there was nothing she and her braves would not do for him. . . . They called Peter the Great White Father, prostrating themselves before him; and he liked this tremendously, so that it was not really good for him. "The Great White Father," he would say to them in a very lordly manner, as they grovelled at his feet, "is glad to see the Piccaninny warriors protecting his wigwam from the pirates." "Me Tiger Lily," that lovely creature would reply, "Peter Pan save me, me his velly nice friend. Me no let pirates hurt him." She was far too pretty to cringe in this way, but Peter thought it his due, and he would answer condescendingly, "It is good. Peter Pan has spoken." (*PP* 91)

In Michael Doyle's extensive study of imperialism, he defines empires as relationships of political control over a people that assume two basic forms: formal, which controls through annexation and rule by a colonial governor with the collaboration of local elites, and informal, which controls through the collaboration of legally independent but politically dependent indigenous rulers.[30] England relied mainly upon the latter form of imperialism, buttressed by an occasional but strategic use of force (for example, the Opium Wars, suppression of the Indian Mutiny, and its blockade of the River Plate),[31] and it is precisely this political paradigm that Barrie's text helps empower. If control is evidenced by the behavioral effects it exerts on those who are controlled, then Peter's control of Tiger Lily textually reproduces the paternalistic ideology at the heart of England's colonialist project and the imperialist ideology at the heart of its paternalism. Like the "piccaninny," Peter's signifier of "Great White Father" tightly imbricates the dominating hierarchies of both colonizer and patriarch into an overdetermined articulation of nationalist interests and, in so doing, pierces the density of the institutions, rituals, and practices that disseminate colonialist discourses.

GEOPOLITICS IN THE "REAL" NEVER-NEVER LAND

The *we*, which articulates natural philosophical consciousness with each other . . . is the unity of absolute knowledge and anthropology, of God and man, of onto-theo-teleology and humanism. "Being" and language—the group of languages—that the *we* governs or opens: such is the name of that which assures the transition between metaphysics and humanism via the *we*.

Jacques Derrida, "The Ends of Man"

We of the Never-Never, Mrs. Aeneas Gunn's diary of a year in the Australian outback, continues to map the discursive terrain that we began exploring in chapter 3 by uncovering the asymmetries of power and subject positions mediated and produced within articulatory practices. At first glance, the "we" of Mrs. Gunn's title and her declaration in the Prelude that "All of Us . . . shared each other's lives for one bright, sunny year" suggest a mutuality which contravenes the coerciveness of the discourses explored in *Peter Pan*. Since the territory of the cattle station Elsey included not only its Anglo-European settlers but also a once independent Aboriginal group who now labored as indentured servants, one begins to grasp the enormous claim implied by Mrs. Gunn's first-person plural pronoun. Without necessarily supporting a "universal pragmatics," or reconstructing the universally valid bases of speech, the "we" of *We of the Never-Never* constructs a localized version of what Jürgen Habermas identifies as "an ideal speech situation." Such a situation creates mutual understanding between participants because it allows its participants equal chances to employ

speech acts, recognizes the legitimacy of each to engage in dialogue as an autonomous and equal partner, and reaches consensus
simply through the better argument.[32] According to Habermas,
"Agreement arrived at through communication, which is measured by the intersubjective recognition of validity claims, makes
possible a networking of social interactions and lifeworld contexts. Of course, these validity claims have a Janus face: As claims,
they transcend any local context; at the same time, they have to be
raised here and now and be de facto recognized if they are going
to bear the agreement of interaction participants that is needed
for effective cooperation."[33]

The signifying practice of *We of the Never-Never* bequeaths us
the first clue about what this claim might be. If a title not only
figures a beginning but also binds its own utterance to the con-
tingency of that which follows,[34] then "The Unknown Woman"—
Mrs. Gunn's first chapter heading—implodes the inclusiveness
of the text's primary title. Instead of a We, where the collective
knows every person, the presence of an unknown divides We into
Us and Them: "us" inside the Never-Never and "them" outside
of it. The "Unknown Woman" refers in this case to the newlywed
Mrs. Gunn, who has followed her husband to his position as man-
ager of the Elsey, and who ascribes her status to the obvious fact
that "everyone . . . was blissfully unconscious of even the existence
of the Maluka's [Mr. Gunn's] missus."[35] Her "unknown" status
also exists as a prerequisite for the claim of the bushmen that the
Never-Never should remain the privileged territory of the Anglo-
European male. As one of the men so baldly pronounces: the cattle
station is "not a fit place for a woman, and besides, nobody wants
her!" (*WNN* 9).

The whitemale crew of the Elsey work feverishly to make sure
that Mrs. Gunn never enters their world by attempting to "block"
her arrival at the Elsey: "The Sanguine Scot had been thinking
rapidly, and, with characteristic hopefulness, felt he had the bull
by the horns. 'We'll just have to block her, chaps; that's all,' he
said. 'A wire or two should do it'; [he] led the way to the telegraph office; and presently there quivered into Darwin the first
hint that a missus was not wanted at the Elsey" (*WNN* 2). The

men of the Elsey tax their imaginations to the limit in their attempts to "block" the "missus." First, they "would advise leaving wife behind till homestead can be repaired" (*WNN* 2). When his wife stands firm in her decision and the Maluka requests a buggy, they reply that no buggy is available, not to mention no sidesaddle and no suitable stock horses. Further, no woman in her right mind would want to travel in the rainy season, and even if she did, "she'll be bored to death if she does reach the homestead alive" (*WNN* 3).

This resistance is particularly interesting from the standpoint of discourse because the attempted exclusion takes place over the Darwin–Pine Creek telegraph lines. In this passage, the telegraph functions as an extremely appropriate trope of discourse: just as the telegraph transmits messages between a sender and a receiver, discourse stresses meaning as communication; just as the Darwin–Pine Creek telegraph facilitates a particular historical and political goal—in this case, the "civilization" of Australia's last frontier and the colonization of Aboriginal lands—discourse operates for particular ideological ends; and just as the Elsey's crew transforms the telegraph into the site of a sexual struggle for power, discourse often becomes a site of ideological domination. As a metadiscourse—that is, a discourse about discourse—this not so innocent act of communication rips apart the consensual fabric from which *We of the Never-Never* weaves its textuality.

In fact, the strenuous endeavors of the bushmen to "unknow" Mrs. Gunn systematically distort the ideal speech situation that *We of the Never-Never* initially presents to the reader. From the earlier thought of Habermas, the concept of systematically distorted communication draws on the methodology of psychoanalysis and illuminates the significance of behavior that has been deformed by repression or censorship: "The psychically most effective way to render undesired need dispositions harmless is to *exclude from public communication* the interpretations to which they are attached—in other words, *repression*." [36] This exclusion of undesired voices from public communication has historically functioned as one of the most potent weapons in the maintenance of power—men over women, colonizer over colonized, white over black. Indeed, the interpretive gloss that the Maluka places on the behavior of his crew vividly dramatizes how pervasive such repression can be: "The Unknown Woman is brimful of possibilities to a bushman . . . for although she may be all womanly strength and tenderness, she may also be anything, from a weak timid fool to a self-righteous shrew, bristling with virtue and indignation. Still . . . when a woman does come into our lives, whatever type she may be, she lacks nothing in the way of chivalry, and it rests with her whether she remains an outsider or becomes just One of Us" (*WNN* 5). While the Maluka characterizes the situation as one that offers a genuine choice, it actually presents Mrs. Gunn with only one desirable course of action: to identify with the bush's dominant masculine community or else be exiled to its social and communicative margins. In this respect, Mrs. Gunn's position exhibits a common female dis-ease whose pathology includes expulsion from conversational communities solely on the basis of gender. Like most women under Western patriarchy, Mrs. Gunn is known but not knowing; seen but not seeing; repressed and Signified but unable herself to participate in these operations.[37]

It is precisely this power-induced asymmetry that systematically distorts *We of the Never-Never*'s initial ideal speech situation, and as in *Peter Pan*, the discourse of the "piccaninny" intervenes to uncover the contradictions of Mrs. Gunn's oppression. In her memoirs, Mrs. Gunn adopts the articulating practice of the Never-Never's white community by substituting the generic "piccaninny" for the individual identities of the Aboriginal children living on the Elsey: "He [the Maluka] reduced the house staff to two, allowing a shadow or two extra in the persons of a few old blackfellows and a piccaninny or two, sending the rejected to camp" (*WNN* 47). As we have seen, the rhetoric of difference that spawns the "piccaninny" functions as an integral part of the Anglo-European imperialist project, and its discursive usage implies participation not only in the discourse itself but also in the sociopolitical privilege it bestows upon its users.

Such participation is paradoxical in Mrs. Gunn's case, however, for although she benefits from the discourse of white privilege, its racist figures turn back on her and literally keep the "missus" in a lower social position. Soon after her own use of "piccaninny," for example, the Maluka describes his wife as "a poor homeless little mite," and she thereafter becomes known to all as "the little Missus." One could loosely write the enthymeme this way:

Premise I: The Missus is a woman.
(Suppressed) Premise II: Women and piccaninnies are little.
Conclusion: The Missus is a piccaninny.

While it is true that standing on her tiptoes, Mrs. Gunn could not have measured much over five feet, her characterization as "little"—the etymological root of "piccaninny"—goes far beyond any spatial definition. Instead, it marks one who is dominated and colonized, whose lower/higher relationship to discourse infers nothing less than that of inferior to superior, oppressed to oppressor.

The "piccaninny" conjures this system of distorted communication because it attempts to conceal the logic of whitemale supremacy in which it is embedded. As David Silverman and Brian Torode explain in *The Material Word: Some Theories of Language and Its Limits*, "Where the sociality of linguistic practice is concealed or fixed in some apparently fixed natural order, we have distorted communication."[38] Mrs. Gunn thus deceives herself about the mutuality, equality, and reciprocity of the linguistic and social "we" that the unknown woman and the known men of the bush create. However, her growing powers of self-reflection ultimately enable her to penetrate the "piccaninny's" ideological veil. Indeed, she laments, "the mistress had long ceased to be anything but the little Missus—something to rule or educate or take care of, according to the nature of her subordinates" (*WNN* 94).

Mrs. Gunn's liberatory self-reflection not only ruptures the bush's systematically distorted communication but also exposes the weakness of one of the most influential contemporary analytics of power—Michel Foucault's elaboration of "fellowships of discourse." According to Foucault, fellowships of discourse preserve or reproduce discourses so that they will circulate within a closed community without those in possession of them becoming dispossessed.[39] Although these fellowships assume myriad forms, they all share schemas of exclusivity and disclosure and a "secret-appropriation and non-interchangeability." Further, they all require a speaking subject (the position from which power/knowledge is exercised) and a spoken subject (the position brought into existence through the exercise of power/knowledge).

However, the positions generated by *We of the Never-Never*'s discursive grid belie these sharp distinctions: although the Maluka and his fellow bushmen appropriate the stance of speaking subjects, the long-suffering Mrs. Gunn simultaneously inhabits the position of both speaking and spoken subject. Foucault's schema fails to account for the contradictory worlds and selves set into play by colonialist discourse itself.[40] According to Habermas, Foucault's "speaking subjects are either masters or shepherds of their linguistic systems. Either they make use of language in a way that is creative of meaning, to disclose their world innovatively, or they are always already moving around within a horizon of world-disclosure taken care of by language itself."[41] The overdetermined status of one who both participates in and is excluded from colonizing discourse eludes his sharply dichotomized positions. Further, in spite of the bushmen's attempts to "block" her from their territory and fellowship of discourse, Mrs. Gunn resists their arguments and, like Wendy, transgresses the boundaries of the Never-Never's rugged and forbidding No (wo)Man's Land. Mrs. Gunn's historical experience requires us to look beyond binary opposition and grasp the multiplicity of positions and contradiction of responses generated by the communicative interaction of the bush.

By arguing for the importance of discourses to Marxist analysis, I do not mean to imply that the material bases for these discourses are at best unimportant or at worst unnecessary. This is an idealist abyss into which too many theorists have fallen—although doubting the reality of the base means that their superstructural fall never comes to a concrete and finite end. The two interpretive poles for any discussion of the relationship between discourse and its material base are two versions of cause and effect: either an unmediated base causes the effects of discourse (vulgar Marxism), or discourse causes the effects of the base (conservative versions of deconstruction). Neither of these positions accurately characterizes the very complex and overdetermined symbiosis between discourse and reality.

In her essay "Histoire d'O: The Construction of a Female Subject," Kaja Silverman suggests that the concept which most accurately characterizes the relationship between real and discursive bodies is that of *anaclisis*.[42] From the Greek verb εϕκλῖυω ("to lean on or upon"), the concept of anaclisis was first articulated by Sigmund Freud as a process in which the sexual instincts satisfy themselves through a propping upon or "leaning up against" the self-preservative instincts.[43] Silverman argues that in an analogous way, discursive bodies lean upon real ones: "lean both in the sense of finding their physical support in, and of exerting their own pressure upon, real bodies. Thus real bodies are tied to, and in the process shaped by, discursive formations."[44] In this ideological symbiosis, discourse territorializes and then maps meaning onto bodies[45]—a description more than faintly reminiscent of nineteenth-century imperialism.

The discourse of the "piccaninny" found its original material support in the European conquest of the West Indies, and it helped to enable this territorialization by mapping the binary oppositions high/low, adult/child, culture/nature, light/dark, and superior/inferior onto European/"native" bodies, respectively. In the colonialist version of anaclisis, then, the interpretation of the "native" Other as childish, dark, and inferior in turn supported Europe's occupation of foreign lands and its paternalistic deracination of their indigenous peoples. Further, as the "piccaninny" became more widely disseminated within the Anglo-European grammar of power, its discourse of difference bound racial and sexual inferiority together through articulating practices such as those we have explored in *Peter Pan* and *We of the Never-Never*. Such are the lessons that Never-Never Land teaches its inhabitants at a very early age.

"Second to the right, and straight on 'til morning." Both the "make-believe" Never-Never Land of Peter Pan and the "true" one of Mrs. Gunn dramatize some of the most insidious discursive means by which women and people of color are marginalized on the boundaries of society. Indeed, I would hope that our imaginary journey to this fabled country has illuminated the necessity for Marxism to profess the analysis of discourse as an inextricable part of its still powerful materialist analysis of colonialism. Short of developing this more adequate model both for reading differently and for reading difference, it might discover second to the right; it will, however, never go straight on 'til morning and complete the journey to a revolutionary, postcolonial methodology.

5

A Passage to
"India"

*Aziz: They all become exactly the same. I give any Englishman
two years.*
Mahmoud Ali: The women are worse.
Aziz: I give them six months.
            David Lean's A Passage to India

The British Raj: the very name conjures images of romance—
"beautiful families, titled friends, and lazy golden afternoons."[1]
Even the creative team for Ralph Lauren's Home Furnishings
division paid homage to this association when it transformed
Anglo-America's recent nostalgia for the "colonial romance" into
an extremely lucrative commodity. Their Polo Home Furnishings
store on Beverly Hills' Rodeo Drive reproduces the very visions
of empire that have enthralled millions of spectators in such films
as *Out of Africa* and *The Jewel in the Crown* in hopes of convinc-
ing buyers that if they purchase the replicated interior of a Raj
family dwelling, they would also purchase its "idyllic" life.[2] Like

many other segments of our society, then, American consumerism not only passively ignores but also actively exploits what Edward Said has called "the evil and utter madness of imperialism."[3] However, the assumption by Polo Home Furnishings' creative directors that "the New York store is a British men's club in a big city, so ours [the Rodeo Drive Polo] should be a British men's club in a more casual environment, like the colonies of the British West Indies, India and Africa,"[4] ironically raises a profoundly important political issue. In addition to its stunning description of colonized cultures as "casual" environments, my attention was riveted by the characterization of Anglo-European imperialism as a "men's club," prompting the question of whether it is true that, in perpetuating empire, women need not apply.

One difficulty in answering this question stems from a conception of colonialist power that remains too dependent on positing direct forms of domination. While colonizing nations certainly did employ military or economic coercion to secure and maintain access to satellite markets, they also penetrated colonized societies by means of signifying *practices*, or the production of meaning-effects, perceptions, self-images, and subject positions necessary to sustain the colonialist enterprise.[5] As Pierre Bourdieu remarks in his *Outline of a Theory of Practice*, such practices ensure that "domination no longer needs to be exerted in a direct, personal way when it is entailed in possession of the means (economic or cultural capital) of appropriating the mechanisms of the field of production and the field of cultural production, which tend to assure their own reproduction by their very functioning, independently of any deliberate intervention by the agents."[6] I will explore the question of empire as a fictional "men's [or women's] club" by analyzing how the signifying practices of empire infiltrate even the intimate psycho-biographical fields of desire—lover for beloved, self for other, Occident for Orient—in *A Passage to India*, David Lean's 1984 filmic rendering of E. M. Forster's 1924 novel. To "India," then, we must direct our spectatorial gaze.

Every European traveler or resident in the Orient has had to protect himself from its unsettling influences. . . . In most cases, the Orient seemed to have offended sexual propriety; everything about the Orient . . . exuded dangerous sex, threatened hygiene and domestic seemliness with an excessive "freedom of intercourse," as [Edward William] Lane put it more irrepressibly than usual.

Edward Said, *Orientalism*

A Passage to India begins its saga with the hypnotically monotonous drum of rain cascading off British umbrellas. The opening frames numb our sight as well, for they paint their visual images from a palette of dull blacks, muted charcoals, and watery grays. Dreary, restrained, and asexual: such is London, the heart of King Edward's empire, in the year 1928. Our first glimpse of Miss Adela Quested (Judy Davis), one of the film's two central female characters, reinforces the reality-effect of England as physically and psychologically drab, for she is swathed in brown, or "neutral" tones as the creative directors for Ralph Lauren might say. She enters the Peninsula and Oriental Steam Navigation Company office to buy passage to India—a journey that she hopes will deliver her not only to a fiancé but also to unknown and eagerly anticipated romantic adventures. While waiting for the clerk to write out her ticket, Adela is strangely drawn to the portraits of India hanging on the office walls. I use the passive tense advisedly here, for this is how the film initially presents "India" to Adela and, through her, to its viewers. In dramatic contrast to the dark dampness of England, "India" is brilliantly sunlit and "naturally" elicits a strong response from Adela. The painting of the Marabar caves—represented as suggestively erotic dark holes leading into the recesses of the Marabar Hills—particularly arrests Adela's gaze; indeed, she can manage only a strangled "I see" in reply to the clerk's observation that these caves are located a mere twenty miles from her own destination.

One might ask why the film employs such a visually exaggerated opposition between England and India to frame its narrative, with the resultant effect of constructing India as an object of intense

desire both for Adela and, vicariously, for the cinematic spectator. We discover an important clue in *A Passage to India*'s initial
presentation of "India" as a painting, that is, as a signifier which
implies the signified as a unified and organic entity capable of
being desired. Of course, such an entity is completely illusory, for
a univocal "India" is an artificial construct with little or no relation to the extraordinarily diverse geographic, ethnic, linguistic,
and religious groups inhabiting its borders.[7] In terms of imperialist processes, however, this fiction possesses strategic value for the
creation and maintenance of an exotic Other as an object of desire
that legitimates the "civilizing" presence of the Western colonizer.
If, as Leo Bersani claims in his work on character and desire, no
psychology is apolitical and every theory of mind has a strategic
value for the culture in which it is developed, might not one say
the same for the economy of desire?[8]

As we have seen, *A Passage to India* begins assigning value
within its economy of desire from the first frames of the film.
This differential continues during Adela and Mrs. Moore's (Dame
Peggy Ashcroft) five-thousand-mile journey, which provides both
a literal passage to the British Civil Service district of Chandrapore and a hermeneutic "*distribution* of geopolitical awareness."[9]
The primary cinematic vehicle for this investment in a whole series
of sociocultural interests is an Eisensteinian montage technique
that juxtaposes shots of the British *vraisemblance*, or semblance
of a society's "natural" attitude, with those it marks as Indian.

For example, the binary opposition order/chaos is mapped onto
British and Indian realities through the sequence of shots an-
nouncing the ship's docking in Bombay. The Viceroy, the historical
figurehead of the Anglo-Indian empire who has traveled to India
on the same ship as Adela and Mrs. Moore, disembarks before
any of the regular passengers. The scene of his entry into port
offers a highly regimented reality: neatly spaced troops listening to
crisply barked orders modulate into a long shot of the Viceroy and
Vicereine framed by the highly symmetrical walls of a triumphal
arch. Quattrocentric codes of scenographic space dominate this
frame, for they place the spectator's eye at the central point of
perspective and allow it to absorb a perfectly ordered figure of
British authority.

This eye match effectively forges a connection between the British filmic presence and a civilizing order. In his collection of essays on *Questions of Cinema*, Stephen Heath illuminates this dynamic through what he calls "the stake of the frame": "The frame is the reconstitution of the scene of the signifier, of the symbolic, into that of the signified, the passage through the image from other scene to seen; it ensures distance as correct position, the summit of the eye, *representation*; it redresses . . . reality and meaning, is the point of their match."[10] This bond is even more strongly cemented by what Heath describes as passing through the image from other scene to seen. The spectator moves from the other scene of Britain as the repository of order—the stately procession of the Viceroy's carriage—to the seen—a teaming mass of "Indians" shouting and waving at the ship. Because it possesses no discernible order, the composition of this shot totally fractures the classical perspectival codes that so precisely center our gaze upon England. The entire frame is filled with bodies crushed together so closely that they seem to rupture its boundaries. Further, while the scenes of the Viceroy's arrival arrange one's gaze as a spectator at a window, the high-to-low passage from scene to seen hierarchically orders our angle of vision on India. This high (British spectator)/ low (Indian spectacle) camera angle carries the ideological effect of order (Britain) gazing upon chaos (India). Even in its beginning moments, then, the signifying practices of *A Passage to India* not only perpetuate but also construct the colonialist image of "India" as a cauldron of anarchic eros and as the exotic Other for the West's voyeuristic eye.

One of the most important literary sites for England's exotic idea of "India" was nineteenth-century popular culture. For example, Robert Southey's poem, *The Curse of Kehama* (1810), narrates the tale of an Indian hero who overthrows a cruel Oriental despot and exhibits a distinctly Western urge for an individualist form of moral and political freedom.[11] Thomas Moore's 1817 *Lallah Rookh*, romantic poems of the daughter of a Mughal emperor and her love for both a poet and a prince, sold out as soon as it appeared in print and was republished innumerable times in the course of the century.[12] To Moore and his enamored public, "India" connoted a dazzling and magical land reminiscent of Coleridge's fabulous Xanadu: "The settings of Moore's stories were glittering palaces and temples and vales and gardens 'rich in eternal blooms.' . . . These scenes of perfumed gardens where birds nested high in the budding cinnamon under 'Araby's soft sun' could shift to scenes of violence and horror, where emotional agony, incredibly fierce and sanguinary battles, horrible chasms and precipices, and terrific tempests surrounded the romantic actors of Moore's action."[13] Although Moore himself had never been to India, he was confident that this mythological color represented an accurate portrait of its society. Even more suggestively for our purposes, his knowledge of "India" frequently came to him in daydreams[14]—those imaginary scenes where the subject is the protagonist and where wishes are fulfilled, albeit in a distorted manner.[15] It seems no coincidence that the primary function of fantasy, according to French psychoanalysts Laplanche and Portalis, is to situate desire.[16]

DESIRE AS METONYMY

If India is the metaphoric equivalence, authorizing the appropriation and naturalization of other cultures, then India is also the repetitive process of metonymy recognized only in its remnants that are, at once, the signs of disturbance and the supports of colonial authority.

Homi K. Bhabha, "Articulating the Archaic:
Notes on Colonial Nonsense"

A Passage to India continues the tradition of Moore with its own version of the Orientalist fantasy: the thousand-mile train journey that carries Adela and Mrs. Moore into the heart of "India's" forbidden territory. This filmic daydream embodies E. M. Forster's own description of India's beckoning to the conquerors: "She calls 'Come.' . . . But come to what? She has never defined. She is not a promise, only an appeal."[17] The film begins to answer the question "coming to what?" in its adoption of director David Lean's favorite parallel montage technique that juxtaposes the story of Adela and Mrs. Moore's introduction to Anglo-Indian society to that of Adela's growing attraction to "India." Using four pairs of similarly structured shots, the parallel montage crosscuts from scenes enclosed within the interior of the train (the "British" reality) to panoramic scenes of the train chugging across the vast desert (the "Indian" reality). The ideological function of this montage takes form in the dialectical relation of the first crosscut pair.

After boarding the train bound for Chandrapore, Adela and Mrs. Moore relax in their compartment by taking tea. They are visited by Mrs. Turton, the overbearing wife of the "Burra Sahib"—the district's chief tax collector—who invites the women for "a drink or something later, after you've recovered." The scene of these four characters at the elegantly furbished dining car table is the first shot of the montage, and the dinner conversation, its answering volley. At one point, Mrs. Turton seconds her husband's commendation of "Ronny's" progress by remarking that he had become a "proper sahib" and was "just the type we want if I might say so." Adela (Ronny's fiancé) looks quite distressed at this news, and during the ensuing silence, the soundtrack fills the conversational lull with noises that initially simulate the rhythm of train wheels but quickly metamorphose into an urgent, insatiable throbbing. This metamorphosis takes place just as the train crosses a bridge, and with it, both Adela and the spectator also cross a signifying bridge into the geopolitical distribution of "India" as a colonized metonymy of desire.

Obviously dismayed at the news that Ronny had become a proper sahib, Adela longs for the eroticism and sensuality—signified in the film by the train's throbbing—that she now suspects will be absent from their marital relationship. In the only rupture of the montage's symmetry, the spectator is first sutured into Adela's perspective as she withdraws from the implications of Mrs. Turton's remark by looking out of the window of the train at the mysteriously lovely scene of light and water. The film then jumpcuts to a long shot in which the train becomes only a small dot within the panorama of "India's" bewitching beauty.

The crosscut between the claustrophobic chattiness of a first-class British dining car and what the jacket of the film video trumpets as a "lush and breathtaking" presentation of India's natural landscape offers an almost Eisensteinian use of montage in the new ideas it creates from the collision of these cultural realities and cinematic contradictions. Beyond the reiteration of a Britain=culture, India=nature dichotomy, the significance of these frames lies in their sequence: we watch Adela's discomfort with the discovery of Ronny as a proper sahib; next, we hear the sound of the train connected to this discomfort and then its metamorphosis into a throbbing; with the throbbing as accompaniment, we then stand in for Adela as she gazes out of the window at the bridge and the moonlit water beyond; finally, we glimpse the train chugging across the bridge from a vast, sweeping distance.

The metonymic structure of desire within this sequence becomes exceedingly clear, for if desire is created by absence, then the montage exposes Adela's displacement of her largely unacknowledged desire from Ronny onto "India." As Kaja Silverman remarks in *The Subject of Semiotics*, "Displacement can only occur between two terms which are either similar or contiguous. Thus desire is in effect nothing more than a series of metaphors and metonymies, displacement away from an unconscious point of origin in which one term replaces another which it either resembles or adjoins." [18] The seductiveness of the second shot, in which the camera lingers on the moonlit body of "India" just as a man's look might linger on the body of a beautiful woman, attests not only to the presence of desire but also to that which transmits this desire—the gaze of the colonizer upon the colonized. The next parallel montage illustrates this point with vivid clarity. After the long river shot, the film again focuses upon the enclosed dining car and Mrs. Moore's request to meet "socially, as friends" some Indians with whom the Turtons are acquainted. An uncomfortable silence ensues. Mr. Turton eventually mumbles that, although he is sure Indians possess all the virtues, they just do not see any socially. Like Adela's response to the thought of Ronny as a proper sahib, Mrs. Moore exhibits distress at this evidence that the Turtons accept racial segregation. Mrs. Turton again seconds her husband's opinion with the comment: "East is East, Mrs. Moore. It's a question of culture." This statement of an absolute "Indian" ontology legitimates racial difference in the way statements of women's ontology have legitimated sexual difference: the ahistorical determinism of both support the oppressive structures of their respective imperialist and patriarchal cultures. Significantly, it is precisely at this point that the film crosscuts to another panoramic view of "India's" implied ontological body: a vast expanse of desert surrounded by mountains and traversed by the tiny figure of the train.

In its photographic quality and exquisite framing by the sculpture of a warrior on horseback, this shot repeats the quattrocentric codes of perspective so characteristic of the film's "British" point of view. Stephen Heath notes that the ideological force of such scenographic space exists in the "image that carries over into a suggestion of the world as a kind of . . . spectacle to be recorded in its essence in an instantaneous objectification for the eye . . . a world, that is, conceived outside of process and practice, empirical scene of the confirmed and central master-spectator, serenely 'present' in tranquil rectilinearity." [19] In this case, however, the central master-spectator is also the colonizer, whose gaze objectifies the marginalized and colonized spectacle. As many feminists have observed, looking and the quality of "to-be-looked-at-ness" do not exist in a vacuum but instead signify states of power and powerlessness. In her fascinating study *Female Desires: How They Are Bought, Sold, and Packaged*, Rosalind Coward contends that "the ability to scrutinize is premised on power. Indeed the look confers power; women's inability to return such a critical and aggressive look is a sign of subordination, of being the recipients of another's assessment." [20] Just as women are objectified by their inability to return the masculinist gaze, "India" cannot return the colonizer's gaze when it is fetishized and subordinated as erotic Nature. Construed by cinematic characters and spectators as an object of desire, "India" beckons like the enchantress Circe to her unwary suitors, and they share with Homer's companions a similar ignominious fate.

Of course, Adela does not literally turn into a swine (the fate of Homer's men); she is only perceived as one by the Indian community when she presses rape charges against Dr. Aziz and by the British when she renounces them. More importantly, I would argue that Adela's accusation of attempted rape culminates the film's primary and secondary processes of desire. In order to fully understand this, however, we need to return to the train journey—or more particularly, to its ending in Chandrapore. After *A Passage to India*'s foreplay of parallel montage, Adela's reunion with her fiancé represents a painfully inadequate resolution of the erotic tension. Ronny greets this woman who has arduously traveled over five thousand miles to marry him with an awkward peck on the cheek and shows more genuine enthusiasm for joining Mr. Turton's reception line. Compared with the eroticism of "India," Ronny's gestures seem small indeed.

The Marabar caves resurface in the view from the veranda of Fairholme, Ronny's microcosm of a bourgeois English estate. He disinterestedly affirms that the mountains Adela glimpses are indeed the Marabar Hills—an acknowledgment that causes her to murmur in a voice dusky with mystery, "and the caves." With an overlap time of several seconds, this frame dissolves into the next shot of Adela sitting on her bed waiting for Ronny to say good night. We watch her brighten with expectation as he approaches and then perceive her dismay as she receives only a restrained "good night, dear," through the bedroom door. At this point, the scene ends with Adela studying her reflection in the mirror. This particular activity subsequently becomes extremely important, since it is repeated when Adela studies her image on the polished walls of the Marabar caves.

While the parallel montage of the train journey exposes the film's metonymic displacement of desire onto "India," the arrival sequence illuminates its overdetermination. The dissolve between the above frames acts, in the words of Louis Althusser, as "the point where several contradictions *condense*—'fuse'—so that this point becomes the *fusion* point—the critical point—the point of revolutionary *mutation*, of '*recrystallization*.'"[21] In the film, this dissolve—the condensing of Adela's unfulfilled eroticism and fascination with "India"—overdetermines her desire. Indeed, its fusion of Adela on the veranda glancing back at the caves and Adela sitting on the bed intertwines such heterogenous contradictions as the British sexual economy of propriety and patriarchy, the socioliterary discourses of "India" as romantic Nature, and the positions of colonizing speaking subject and colonized spoken object within the thick tissue of *A Passage to India*'s cinematic text. It is this overdetermination that also stimulates the growth of secondary trajectories of desire from a primary root. If displacement involves the actual substitution of one object for another and the involvement of the original object in a series of new signifying transactions, then secondary trajectories greatly extend the network of these transactions through the creation of multiple displacements.[22]

In *A Passage to India*, one of the most important secondary trajectories is embodied in the figure of Dr. Aziz (Victor Banerjee), whom the narrator in E. M. Forster's novel describes as "an athletic little man, daintily put together, but really very strong."[23] Dr. Aziz's pivotal role stems from the fact that in the latter half of the film, Adela withdraws the cathection of her desire from "India" and transfers it to him—a process set into motion by her experience in the ruined temple. After bicycling several miles outside of Chandrapore, Adela comes upon a weed-choked pathway and the crumbling walls of an ancient edifice. Deciding to investigate, she follows the path until she stumbles across the remains of what had obviously been the entrance to a Hindu temple. The music here repeats the overture's opening theme and orchestrates it with reed instruments, which are often the West's musical evocation of the mysteriousness of the East. However, the ethereality of the reeds sounds a threatening note, and we, along with Adela, discover the reason in the next sequence of frames: within the temple ruins, male and female figures lie embracing in various degrees of sexually explicit poses. While for most sects of Hinduism, these figures manifest both the presence of cosmogonic beings (especially Siva and Parvati) and the continuing fertility of the earth, for Adela they manifest only the terror of her own displaced desire. The film thus shrouds the incident within the veils of that dangerous sexuality which Edward Said claims is so characteristic of Orientalism.

This construction of "India" as a site of dangerous, almost bestial, sexuality is reinforced by the inhabitation of the temple by a group of very large and hostile monkeys. They charge Adela, who hastily retreats to escape not only the monkeys but also the rampant sensuality of the temple. If, as Mrs. Moore remarked earlier, India "forces one to come face to face with oneself," Adela's disturbing experience at the temple marks her refusal to do so. Upon returning to Chandrapore, she retracts her decision not to marry Ronny, for a "proper" Anglo-Indian marriage brings safety, security, and boundaries to contain any propensity toward anarchic eroticism. Adela's refusal to confront her desire sets its secondary displacement into motion, and this process has potentially tragic consequences for Dr. Aziz.

Too many discussions of Adela's profound trauma in the Marabar caves and her subsequent rape charge against Aziz have focused on the alleged pathologies of her sexuality. This tendency to privatize her experience recirculates a Western individualist psychology and, in fact, obscures the way in which even the most intimate objects of desire are ideologically cathected (women fetishized within patriarchal societies have known this for centuries). To paraphrase a statement by Michel Foucault, the central issue is not to determine whether Adela says yes or no to her own sexuality; rather, it is "to discover who does the speaking, the positions and viewpoints from which they speak, the institutions which prompt people to speak about it and which store and distribute the things that are said. What is at issue, briefly, is the over-all 'discursive fact,' the way in which sex is 'put into discourse.'"[24] A Passage to India puts Adela's primary desire into discourse through the binary oppositions that Victorian-Edwardian colonialism and her desire for Aziz share.

Adela's focus on Aziz begins, appropriately enough, with another train journey and a secondary passage to India—this time to the Marabar Hills. However, on this journey, the intense throbbing of the train has metamorphosed into the rhythmic jangle of an elephant's bells, and the elegantly cool dining car, into a spectacularly barren and searingly hot stone mountain. Adela and Mrs. Moore accompany Dr. Aziz on an elaborately arranged picnic to the hills. After an attack of claustrophobia in one of the lower caves, Mrs. Moore encourages her two companions to proceed alone to the upper ones that supposedly possess an even more striking capacity for echoes. In a moment of rest from this rather strenuous climb, Adela and Aziz stop to admire the dramatic view of Chandrapore from the top of the hills. Interestingly enough, these are the only frames where the camera completely sutures the spectator into the perspective of a specific character: we look with Adela as she peers through her binoculars, trying to bring Chandrapore and its inhabitants into focus. While this might seem innocuous enough, it represents A Passage to India's literal and symbolic differentiation of only the Western gaze. We are never allowed to perceive India through non-Western eyes; when the film does present Indian characters, they are always filtered through the camera's Anglo-European lens—just as Forster's novel filters its narrative through an obviously British consciousness.

This pattern perpetuates *A Passage to India*'s tendency to inscribe certain features of European colonialism in its specific signifying practices. As Robert Stam and Louise Spence note in their essay "Colonialism, Racism, and Representation: An Introduction," "The magic carpet of these apparatuses flies us around the globe and makes us, by virtue of our subject position, its audiovisual masters. It produces us as subjects, transforming us into armchair conquistadores, affirming our sense of power while making the inhabitants of the Third World objects of spectacle for the First World's voyeuristic gaze."[25] Perhaps surveying the physically distant view of Chandrapore helps Adela achieve some psychological distance from her perplexing concerns, for immediately afterward, she asks Aziz whether he loved his wife when he married her. He answers that, since his marriage was arranged when he was very young, the question hardly seems applicable. But, she persists, what about love? "We were man and woman, and we were young," Aziz replies. This suggestion of sexual passion to a woman who has experienced none is implied in the next scenes of Aziz offering Adela his hand as they climb the steep stairs to the caves. As they approach, the film repeats the same reedlike melody that was used to embed the ruined temple in a context of dangerous and exotic eroticism. The musical score functions like an ideological glue that binds the temple scene with the present context and displaces Adela's desire onto Dr. Aziz as a metonymic representation of "India."

Indeed, both Adela's charge of attempted rape against Aziz and the ensuing trial seem almost inevitable in the face of her unacknowledged desire: "What happened in the caves? *There*, the loss of the narrative of cultural plurality. . . . *There* the enactment of an undecidable, uncanny colonial present, an Anglo-Indian difficulty, which repeats . . . 'Come.' . . . But come to what?"[26] Although he is discussing the transparent assimilation of cross-cultural meanings in some universal human culture, Homi K. Bhabha offers an intriguing framework for the incident in the Marabar caves in his essay "Articulating the Archaic: Notes on Colonial Nonsense." According to Bhabha, Adela "somatizes" her experience in the caves in repeated, hysterical narratives.[27] In yet another metonymical journey down the chain of signifiers, she ultimately displaces her desire onto the very surface of her body, which, "Sebastian-like, is covered in colonies of cactus spines."[28] It is only when the trial forces her to face herself, when "something that she did not understand took hold of the girl and pulled her through,"[29] that Adela breaks the chain of desire. By claiming it as part of her own Imaginary, Adela creates the space for potentially redistributing the psychological relationship between desiring subject and desired object; by rupturing the imperialist production of desire, she abdicates that "flexible positional superiority" upon which Orientalism depends.[30] One could only wish that the creative directors of Ralph Lauren's Home Furnishings had been as honest.

Once the discussion moves beyond the confines of overt domination into the realm of practice, the question raised by women's historical and fictional participation in imperialism becomes sharply focused. *A Passage to India* illustrates the difficulty of extrication from the Anglo-European project because, in spite of an explicitly critical stance, the film's signifying practices mire it even more deeply in colonialism's metonymical muck. Is the Raj a men's club? We must now answer the question with an equivocal "yes and no": yes, in that only British men retained access to its military and economic buttresses; no, in that British women indirectly, and sometimes unwittingly, disseminated structures of cultural signification that supported the entire apparatus. Although both E. M. Forster's novel and David Lean's film give traditionally "fictional" accounts of colonialism, they are, in a profound sense, more accurate than many "factual" accounts, for both enable us to begin unraveling the myriad threads woven into the extraordinarily complex and contradictory text of colonialism.

6

Rereading Moses /
Rewriting Exodus

*It is at the level of the imagination that the fateful issues of our
new world-experience must first be mastered. It is here that culture and history are broken. . . . Old words do not reach across
the new gulfs, and it is only in vision and oracle that we can
chart the unknown and new-name the creatures.*
                    Amos Wilder, Theopoetics

*The promised land is not simply a new country; it is also the gift
of a radically new situation.*
        Gustavo Gutierrez, We Drink from Our Own Wells

In September 1939, *American Home* magazine responded to the
eruption of World War II in Europe by reminding its housewife
readers: "Hitler threatens Europe, but Betty Havens' husband's
boss is coming to dinner—and *that's* what *really* counts."[1] An
unlikely woman resisted such incorrigible innocence and, like the
prophetic Cassandra, raised her voice in witness to "the trail of

bloody guilt" inflicted by the ambitions of imperialism—whether German, Japanese, or American. Although novelist and folklorist Zora Neale Hurston escaped Cassandra's murderous fate for expressing her views, she did suffer a form of cultural violence when Lippincott refused to include her 1941 essay "Seeing the World as It Is" in Hurston's autobiography. Perhaps in the aftermath of Pearl Harbor, her publishers were deterred by the essay's allegation that Japan merely plagiarized from the ditty "we Westerners" composed about trading in China with gunboats and cannons;[2] or perhaps it was her equally bold assertion that, while people shuddered at the thought of Germany collecting taxes in Holland, they refused to utter a word "against Holland collecting one twelfth of poor people's wages in Asia" (*DTR* 342). I suspect, however, that the most subversive element in Hurston's essay was not her criticism of particular countries but her devastating critique of the relationship between nationalism and ethnocentrism: "There is no diffused light on anything international so that a comparatively whole scene may be observed. Light is sharply directed on one spot, leaving not only the greater part in darkness but also denying by implication that the great unlighted field exists" (*DTR* 357).

Hurston struggled painfully with nationalism, which she interchangeably called "Race Pride," "Race Solidarity," and "Race Consciousness." For Hurston, "instead of Race Pride being a virtue, it is a sapping vice. It has caused more suffering in the world than religious opinion, and that is saying a lot" (*DTR* 324). Primarily a cultural phenomenon that often assumes political form, nationalism fans the desire to preserve a people's national or cultural identity when that identity is threatened or to transform or even create it when it is felt to be inadequate or lacking.[3] When Hurston declares that "Race Pride is a luxury I cannot afford" because there are "too many implications behind the term" (*DTR* 324), she is perceiving the world through a global perspective that rejects the will to organic identity upon which ethnocentrism and nationalism depend—regardless of their origin.

Just as literary organicism establishes an equivalence between processes of natural growth and products of spontaneous creativity,[4] the notion of "organic" identity suggests an essential relation between genetics and social character. It is a totalizing movement whose subject, as Paul de Man observes, claims an "irrational, unmediated experience of particular selfhood (or loss of selfhood)."[5] Within this allegedly unmediated experience, nationalist identity exists as a racially, culturally, and metaphysically pure essence that excludes all other marginal and impure "particular selfhoods." This was certainly the most oppressive process of nationalism in Hurston's own historical era. Indeed, the period between 1918 and 1945—the years in which Hurston wrote "Seeing the World as It Is"—spawned an especially intolerant, inhumane, and violent form of the will to organic identity called national socialism.

In their work *The Genocidal Mentality: Nazi Holocaust and Nuclear Threat*, Robert Jay Lifton and Eric Markusen describe how the Nazi biomedical vision legitimated the ruthless suppression of difference—both political and racial—because it signified an illness that threatened the unity of the indivisible national organism.[6] Concomitantly, the social cultivation and biological propagation of "Aryan" qualities could become the basis for a more vital national identity. No statement more dramatically demonstrates the dangers of such thinking than Hitler's ominous demand that "from a dead mechanism which only lays claim to existence for its own sake, there must be formed a living organism with the exclusive aim of serving a higher idea."[7]

Hurston locates a fertile ground for this will to organic identity in the biblical narrative of the Exodus, which tells the story of how Moses led the Israelite people out of Egypt and into the Promised Land:

> The Old Testament is devoted to what was right and just from the viewpoint of the Ancient Hebrews. All of their enemies were twenty-two carat evil. They, the Hebrews, were never aggressors. The Lord wanted His children to have a country full of big grapes and tall corn. Incidentally, while they were getting it, they might as well get rid of some trashy tribes that He never did think much of, anyway. With all of its figs and things, Canaan was their destiny. God sent somebody especially to tell them about it. If the conquest looked like bloody rape to the Canaanites, that was because their evil

ways would not let them see a point which was right under
their nose. (*DTR* 333)

However, the Exodus has also functioned as an anticolonialist
paradigm for such historically diverse groups as African American
slaves in their resistance to slavery, South American campesinos
in their struggle to overthrow oppressive political regimes, and
southern blacks in their fight for civil rights. As the introduction to
a collection entitled *Exodus—A Lasting Paradigm* asserts: "That
Exodus is a paradigm of lasting importance has everything to do
with the fact that it expresses an experience that is closely related to one of the fundamental and lasting human needs, that of
freedom and independence."[8]

What Hurston objects to is *not* the Exodus story itself, but
rather, a certain supernaturalist interpretation that conceives of
God as completely separate from the world and of finite beings
as existing only through the decision of divine will.[9] In Hurston's
words, if and when "the Lord wanted" a Promised Land for the
ancient Hebrews, it is a totally voluntary act, and nothing prevents God from adopting a stance of hatred or indifference toward
them.[10] According to theologian David Ray Griffin, this model
"provides a necessary support for the ethnocentric view that God,
like humans, loves some beings (us), is indifferent to some others
(those we exploit), and hates still others (our enemies)."[11] It is
precisely this appropriation of the Exodus that Hurston calls into
question: just as the Exodus begins with the civil disobedience
of the Hebrew midwives Shiphrah and Puah, Hurston commits
civil disobedience against her own African American and Christian traditions by rewriting the Exodus in the too often neglected
novel, *Moses, Man of the Mountain* (1939).[12]

Even though it lacks the artistic exquisiteness of *Their Eyes
Were Watching God*, *Moses* is in fact a much bolder work whose
1939 publication date demands that we read the biblical story of
the Exodus, Hurston's fictional work of Moses, and the global
theater of a world at war intertextually. In *Moses, Man of the
Mountain*, for example, Moses decries "the intensified nationalism which had been whipped up for a generation by his father.
Egypt was spreading by conquest and alliances based on force. If

Rereading Moses/Rewriting Exodus

105

they didn't keep on getting more they would begin to look weak" (*MMM* 77). The imperialist nationalism of Pharaoh's Egypt could be a model for the machinations of Hitler in Europe and, according to Hurston, England in India, the United States in South America, and the Kings of Dahomey in West Africa.

It is both the content and form of this organic nationalism that Hurston's Moses symbolically annihilates in the well-known story of how he kills the Egyptian foreman:

> He was upon the new public works, a causeway, splendidly conceived, which was being built with forced Hebrew labor. He saw the men straining and striving and the Egyptian bossman striding among them and striking out with his bullwhip without regards to whom he hit nor why. Moses stopped in his tracks and looked on. He looked at the straining backs of the workmen and then at the face of the foreman, and suddenly he saw all Egypt in that face. . . . Moses heard the wails and woke out of his nausea at what he was seeing. He leaped upon the foreman and snatched the whip away. With his right arm, so famous in Asia and Africa, he swung and struck the foreman between the eyes and staggered him. . . . Twice again he struck the creature of Pharaoh's hatred and intolerance and the man lay on the sand without a quiver. Moses stooped down and saw the man was dead. (*MMM* 90)

In Hurston's novel, the context for this killing was Moses' demand that Egypt either restore the enslaved Hebrews to full citizenship or permit them to leave the country. His enemies opposed this demand by questioning Moses' ethnic identity and accusing him of being a despised Hebrew himself. After killing the foreman, Moses visits the tomb of his beloved friend Mentu. " 'Am I a Hebrew?' he asked himself there, but found nothing to convince him that he was" (*MMM* 92).

This question and questioning of identity possesses profound political implications for the appropriation of the Exodus as an anticolonialist paradigm. In the biblical story, for example, Moses' identity as a Hebrew is established beyond any doubt. A Levite woman gives birth to a son whom she hides in order to escape Pharaoh's command to kill all the newborn male infants of the

enslaved Israelites; however, when the baby becomes too difficult
to hide, she places him in a papyrus basket and

> put it among the reeds along the bank of the Nile. His sister
> stood a distance to see what would happen to him.
>
> Then Pharaoh's daughter went down to the Nile to bathe,
> and her attendants were walking along the river bank. She
> saw the basket among the reeds and sent her slave girl to get
> it. She opened it and saw the baby. He was crying and she felt
> sorry for him. "This is one of the Hebrew babies," she said.
>
> Then his sister asked Pharaoh's daughter, "Shall I go and
> get one of the Hebrew women to nurse the baby for you?"
>
> "Yes, go," she answered. And the girl went and got the
> baby's mother. Pharaoh's daughter said to her, "Take this
> baby and nurse him for me, and I will pay you." So the woman
> took the baby and nursed him. When the child grew older,
> she took him to Pharaoh's daughter and he became her son.
> She named him Moses, saying, "I drew him out of the water."
> (Exod. 2:3b–6)

Most biblical scholars attribute this infancy narrative to the
reconstructed source by the anonymous author known as "the
Yahwist," or "J," who between 960 and 930 B.C.E. created a story
of Israel's origins from the world's creation to the entrance of the
Israelites into the Promised Land of Canaan. In *The Hebrew Bible:
A Socio-Literary Introduction*, Norman Gottwald notes that "J"
wrote a kind of "national epic" for the young kingdom of David
and Solomon and exhibited a "national political tone" that dis-
tinguishes it from the Hebrew Bible's other narrative sources.[13]
Clearly, establishing the identity of Moses as a Hebrew was central to such an epic, for tracing its genealogy back through the
founding patriarchs imbued the Israelite nation with a profound
sense of historical, political, and spiritual mission—a sense that
bequeathed to them an almost modern nationalist consciousness.[14]

Moses, Man of the Mountain, on the other hand, contradicts
the Yahwist pericope by allowing the infant's sister Miriam to fall
asleep immediately after she places him in the water. By the time
she wakes up, both baby and basket have disappeared. Although
the reader is told that a boy named Moses lives in the palace as the

son of the princess, she or he can only respond to the question of Moses' identity by reiterating the words of Miriam: "Oh—er—...I don't know." As a Hebrew slave in *Moses* remarks: "If Horus [the Egyptian sun-god] is the weaver of the beginning of things, he's done put some mighty strange threads in his loom" (*MMM* 13). The word "text," of course, derives etymologically from the Latin verb meaning "to weave" or "produce" (texture, textile, tissue). If Hurston is the weaver of a new Exodus, then she—like the sun-god Horus—puts some mighty strange threads in *her* loom of Moses' character, for her text obstructs the decidability of Moses' origins and forces the reader to oscillate between the culturally inculcated belief that he is a Hebrew and the fictional implication that he is an Egyptian. Each perspective questions the other through this undecidable, nonsynthetic oscillation,[15] and the character of Moses produced within it becomes irrevocably marked by a drifting apart within identity, or difference.[16]

Jacques Derrida describes such an aporia with the neologism différance, which combines the two senses of the French verb *différer*—to differ and to defer, to differentiate and to postpone. According to Leslie Wahl Rabine in her provocative article "A Feminist Politics of Non-identity," différance "hovers between a noun form and a verb form, between a spatial and a temporal reference" and "signifies a productive energy and force that produces and continues to work invisibly within the apparently stable and self-identical entities at each pole of an opposition."[17] Transposing différance into Hurston's terms, the oscillation between the character-effect "Moses" and the biblical signifier "Moses"[18] requires the reader to participate in the play of differences that signifies "neither/nor, that is, *simultaneously*, either *or*":[19] neither Hebrew nor Egyptian, that is, simultaneously either Hebrew or Egyptian. Like the phallocentric subject, the nationalist subject depends upon the hierarchies of inside and outside, native and alien, and finds his or her natural habitat in the structure of metaphysical opposition.[20] Moses' ethnic undecidability thus begins to fracture an organic nationalist consciousness and profoundly questions the terms on which the Exodus—the paradigmatic journey of liberation—can be appropriated.

While the Exodus journey is still a journey toward freedom, it is no longer a journey toward unity. If we follow *Moses, Man of the Mountain* on the Exodus journey, we do not enter a Promised Land where a jealous Yahweh commands us to break down the altars, smash the sacred stones, and cut down the Asherah poles of its indigenous peoples (Exod. 34:13); instead, we discover a land whose profound plurivocity acts as an antidote to the poisonous univocity of nationalism and monotheism. We discover a land in which Mount Sinai itself exists as the sacred locus not of Yahweh alone but rather of the new *mestiza*. In *Borderlands/ La Frontera: The New Mestiza*, Gloria Anzaldúa prophesies that "the future will belong to the mestiza. Because the future depends on the breaking down of dominant cultural paradigms, it also depends on the ability to straddle two or more cultures. By creating a new mythos—that is, by a change in the way we perceive reality, the way we see ourselves, and the ways we behave—*la mestiza* creates a new consciousness." [21] *La mestiza* shatters, for example, such entities as a separatist race consciousness since she stands at the confluence of two or more racial/ideological/cultural/biological streams, with chromosomes/ideologies constantly "crossing over." [22] This mixture gives birth to "a mutable, more malleable species with a rich gene pool" [23] and gives new meaning to the pivotal transition of Hurston's Moses—his escape from Egypt by crossing over the Red Sea:

Moses had crossed over. He was not in Egypt. He had crossed over and now he was not an Egyptian. He had crossed over. The short sword at his thigh had a jewelled hilt but he had crossed over and so it was no longer the sign of his high birth and power. He had crossed over, so he sat down on a rock near the seashore to rest himself. He had crossed over so he was not of the house of Pharaoh. He did not own a palace because he had crossed over. He did not have an Ethiopian Princess for a wife. He had crossed over. He did not have friends to sustain him. He had crossed over. He did not have enemies to strain against his strength and power. He had crossed over. He was subject to no law except the laws of tooth and talon. He had crossed over. The sun who was his friend and ancestor in Egypt was arrogant and bitter in Asia.

He had crossed over. He felt as empty as a post hole for he was none of the things he once had been. He was a man sitting on a rock. He had crossed over. (*MMM* 103–4)

When he begins his journey, Moses has no idea where he will go—until he sees his first mountain, that is. The mountain beckons him and offers something for which he has searched all of his life. " 'What is the name of that mountain?' he [Moses] asked the man nearest him. 'It's according to where you live. The people on one side of it call it Horeb. On the other side they call it Sinai' " (*MMM* 111). At first glance, the existence of two names for the same mountain seems merely to echo the Hebrew Bible's own variant naming: Sinai in the Yahwist or "J" source tradition and Horeb in the Elohist or "E" source tradition. Although the Yahwist depicts an actively intervening God who expects from Israel a childlike faith that will bless all nations, and the Elohist, a more reserved deity who communicates through dreams and visions,[24] one cannot construe these differences of style and historical viewpoint as a heterotheistic ethos. The Yahweh/Elohim of Mount Sinai/Horeb still demands that one hold no other gods before him [*sic*] and fiercely defends against the apostasy of his [*sic*] people.

For Hurston's Moses, the mountain "hovered over him and called him as a mother would. He must go up and embrace his mother" (*MMM* 121). Jane Ellen Harrison emphasizes in her pioneering work *Mythology* that the Mountain-Mother is a goddess image of the first importance: "The mountain naturally enough . . . stood for Earth, and the Earth is Mother because she gives life to plants, to animals, to man."[25] This framing of the mountain with the imagery of the goddess continues when Moses journeys toward it and comes to rest under a sycamore tree nestled at its foot. Most of the ancient Mediterranean world, including Egypt, perceived the sycamore tree as the "Living Body of Hathor on Earth." Indeed, the Goddess Hathor—the Eye of Wisdom and the Lady of the Serpent—was also called the Lady of the Sycamore,[26] and some scholars have persuasively linked these sacred sycamore figs to the *asherim* that Yahweh directs his [*sic*] people to cut down.[27] *Moses, Man of the Mountain* once again weaves its text from the threads of *différance*, since Moses—the man of the mountain—must call the mountain both Horeb and Sinai, Mother and Father, simultaneously. Like his ethnic identity, the identity of the sacred becomes undecidable.

The presence of the Goddess emerges most strongly, however, in the second "crossing over" of Moses, namely, the Israelites' escape from Pharaoh by fording the Red Sea. According to Gottwald, the dominant line of biblical interpretation has identified the crossing of the *yâm sup*, the Sea of Reeds, as the nucleus of the Exodus event and therefore of Israel's salvation history.[28] I would argue that this assertion also holds true for Hurston's rewriting of the Exodus, for the Israelites' crossing of the sea allows her to weave the textures of the Goddess into the jealously guarded domain of God. Indeed, Moses envisions the Exodus itself as a progeny of the Cosmic Egg, the Egg of all life—one of the most ubiquitous symbols for the Goddess: "This time he had crossed over safely with a nation behind him and no weapon worth talking about but his right hand. Well, the present was an egg laid by the past that had the future inside its shell" (*MMM* 240).

In *The Chalice and the Blade: Our History, Our Future*, Riane Eisler elucidates the meaning of the Cosmic Egg: "In visual or symbolic terms, this is the representation of power as linking. It has from time immemorial been symbolized by the circle or oval— the Goddess's cosmic egg or Great Round—rather than by the jagged lines of a pyramid where, as gods or as the heads of nations or families, men rule from the top."[29] It is precisely the power of the pyramid and its sociotheological system of male dominance, male violence, hierarchy, and authoritarianism[30] that Moses leaves behind in his first crossing over from Egypt to the Promised Land and that he desires the Israelites to leave behind in the second crossing over. The life-transforming catharsis that he experienced after killing the Egyptian foreman enabled Moses to discover a kind of relationship that is not dependent on sexual, racial, or political domination: " 'I don't want to be anybody's boss. In fact, that is the very thing I want to do away with,' he said quietly" (*MMM* 95). This turn away from dominance and toward the partnership of nature frames and illuminates the affirmation of the Cosmic Egg as the nucleus of the Exodus. This episode reiterates Moses' first crossing over with one crucial difference: whereas the first questions Moses' individual identity and destiny, the second questions the Israelites' national identity and destiny—and, by implication, that of any group which appropriates the Exodus as a liberating paradigm.

Further, this collective crossing over profoundly criticizes the Israelite assertion that "Yahweh is a warrior; Yahweh is his name" (Exod. 15:3)—a critique that catapults Hurston into a direct confrontation not only with biblical tradition but also with such African American freedom movements as Marcus Garvey's 1920s Pan-Africanism. One of the most phenomenal social movements in this century, Garvey's Pan-Africanism built its ideal of freedom upon the foundation of Yahweh as a War Lord. Garvey himself writes that "God is a bold sovereign—a Warrior Lord. . . . He does not allow anything to interfere with His power and authority."[31] Not surprisingly, Garvey's concept of salvation was also grounded upon an admonition to secure power:[32] "POWER is the only argument that satisfies man. Man is not satisfied; neither is he moved by prayers, by petitions, but every man is moved by that *power* of authority which forces him to do, even against his will. . . . The only advice I can give the Negro is to get *power*."[33] Since Garvey was also known as the "black Moses," one can hardly imagine a starker contrast with Hurston's Moses, who repudiates militarism in all its forms: "From now on his sword should cease to think for him. He would spend the rest of his life asking Nature the why of her moods and measures" (*MMM* 101).

The traditional exaltation of Yahweh as a warrior and the inability to separate this image from Yahweh the liberator of the oppressed have caused many contemporary feminist theologians to reject the Exodus as a paradigm of freedom. As Carol P. Christ argues in her *Laughter of Aphrodite: Reflections on a Journey to the Goddess*: "My rejection of this God as a liberating image for feminist theology is based on my understanding of the symbolic function of a warrior God in cultures where warfare is glorified as a symbol of manhood and power. . . . Since liberation theology is fundamentally concerned with the use of biblical symbolism in shaping contemporary reality and the understanding of the divine ground, this method is appropriate. In a world threatened by total nuclear annihilation, we cannot afford a warlike image of God."[34] Almost fifty years before Carol Christ wrote her essay "Why Women Need the Goddess," Zora Neale Hurston had her own doubts about the symbolic function of a warrior God in cultures where the social diseases of imperialism, nationalism, and ethnocentrism infect the most intimate workings of the body politic.

However, this intertwining of the nurturing, life-giving Goddess with the warrior God in *Moses, Man of the Mountain* also questions the pernicious will to organic identity found in much of the contemporary Goddess movement. Christ herself defines the simplest and most basic meaning of the Goddess as the "acknowledgement of the legitimacy of female power as a beneficent and independent power."[35] The use of the word "female" imbues Christ's definition of the Goddess with biological overtones and strongly suggests that, as all women share the capacity to reproduce, all women experience the female body and its life cycle in similar ways. This assumption ignores the way in which women's experience of their bodies is culturally mediated, and Christ's analysis becomes subject to some of the same criticisms of nationalism that Hurston raises in "Seeing the World as It Is." In *The Once and Future Goddess: A Symbol for Our Time*, Elinor Gadon addresses this potential for ethnocentrism in her statement that each woman taps into the power of the Goddess according to her own priorities.[36] Artist Faith Ringgold, for example, responded to the presence of the Goddess in African American experience by creating a series of masks called "Weeping Witches" that mourn black women's double oppression of both racism and sexism.[37] There *is* no universal or natural "female" manifestation of the Goddess; rather, she works through infinitely particular and highly mediated cultural structures.

The concerns that problematize Christ's use of the word "female" also infest her notion of women's power as innately "beneficent." For Christ, this power involves both the creativity of physical birth and the female body as the "*direct* incarnation of waxing and waning, life and death cycles in the universe" (emphasis added).[38] This naturalistic and biologistic language conflates sex with gender and cloaks the fact that "sex/gender systems are not ahistorical emanations of the human mind"—or, in this

case, of the human body; rather, "they are products of historical human activity."[39] As feminist, psychotherapist, and political
theorist Jane Flax notes, men's and women's understanding of biology, sexuality, and reproduction emerges from and must satisfy
or challenge a set of preexisting gender relations.[40] Thus, there
are no "direct" incarnations of physical birth in women's psyches.
Although Christ acknowledges this mediation in analyzing how
a patriarchal culture devalues women's experience, she seems to
forget it during her impassioned discourse on what the Goddess
might mean for women.

The historical context of *Moses, Man of the Mountain* offers an
excellent example of how biological sexuality is always already
transformed by the processes of ideological activity. The most
notorious woman within the Third Reich was Reichsfrauenfüh-
rerin Gertrud Scholtz-Klink, chief of the Women's Bureau. As
Claudia Koonz notes in her cautionary tale of *Mothers in the
Fatherland: Women, the Family, and Nazi Politics*, motherhood
(or, in Christ's terms, women's physical creativity), far from im-
munizing women against evil, "fired women's dedication to the
Führer's vision of an 'Aryan' future and expanded opportunities
for women to reign in their own *Lebensraum* [living room]."[41] To
further this end, according to Koonz, professional women founded
"eugenic" motherhood schools and brides left the labor market
in order to receive state loans for bearing acceptably "Aryan"
children. The anonymous publicist for Scholtz-Klink's book *The
Woman in the Third Reich* perhaps summarizes it best when he or
she promises that these writings will demonstrate how "women
came naturally to form the 'biological middle-point'" of a new
society empowered by "nationalist and racial powers."[42] Far from
being passive or autocolonized victims of masculinism, women in
the Third Reich provided the enabling conditions for a murderous National Socialist state in the name of the physical creativity
called motherhood.[43]

Moses, Man of the Mountain bequeaths us a rich opportunity
for thinking through such difficulties because it forces us to read
against both the patriarchal Western tradition and the will to
organic identity in some feminist theories; in so doing, it clears a
new imaginative space for the oppositional and différant knowl-

edge of the new *mestiza*. Although theologian Karen McCarthy Brown speaks of "radical pluralism" in the following passage, she could also be describing the workings of this new *mestiza* consciousness,

> a style of understanding that holds multiple truths in dynamic tension. . . . If truth begins in experience, then there must be many truths, for there are many life stories and many stories within a single life. Furthermore, many truths, held in creative tension and rooted in the deepest parts of one's being, may better equip one to handle the challenges and dangers of contemporary life than those great philosophical, political, and religious systems that, historically, have been able to define themselves only in opposition to other systems. Radical pluralism is not an easy stance toward the world, for there is no place to go "home" to when the crises of one's life demand security before anything else.[44]

Hurston's text holds its many stories in creative tension by the networks of différance, which enmesh God with Goddess, Egyptian with Hebrew, and produce a textual/theological double-voicedness, a radical pluralism, which a monotheistic ethos abhors.

However, the pluralism of différance is not identical to a political program of pluralism. In *The Post-Colonial Critic: Interviews, Strategies, Dialogues*, Gayatri Spivak remarks that such a program has already shown its "dark side," particularly in the United States, and thus remains a severely limited strategy for any anti-colonialist movement.[45] Although Spivak herself does not further explain these negative qualities, one could point to the fact that conservative intellectual and social factions have thoroughly recuperated pluralism by reducing the potential for disruption in racial, sexual, physical, and cultural difference to the status of benign variation. A libertarian idea of pluralism is also used to resist affirmative-action programs because affirmative action presupposes that we exist as members of unequal groups, whereas libertarian pluralism argues that all individuals should be subject to one standard of judgment.

Feminist sociologist Alice Rossi identifies the sexual politics of bourgeois-libertarian pluralism when she observes: "In the case of sex, the pluralist model posits the necessity of traditional sex role differentiation between the sexes on the grounds of fundamental physiological and hence social differences between the sexes."[46] Thus, both androgyny and sexual difference argue for the complementarity of masculine and feminine gender identity and view their separateness as unproblematic, so long as they are equally valued; once women secure this valuation, they will experience the same liberty and equality as men.[47] Unlike the pluralist model, however, différance discovers "encroachments, overflows, leaks, skids, shifts, slips"[48] in both the narrative text and the text of sexual identity. Like nationality, gender becomes unstable, mobile, and heterogenous—a fluid process of negotiation rather than a rigid imposition of meaning. In his own description of the polyvalent text, Roland Barthes chooses a biblical motto—"My name is legion, for we are many" (Mark 5:9)[49]—which seems especially appropriate for Hurston's critique of the will to organic identity.

The world of the new *mestiza* subverts metaphysical, cultural, and racial boundaries and works against the imperialism of "purity" that has lethally oppressed so much of humankind. As Gloria Anzaldúa so eloquently argues:

> The work of *mestiza* consciousness is to break down the subject-object duality that keeps her a prisoner and to show in the flesh and through the images in her work how duality is transcended. The answer to the problem between the white race and the colored, between males and females, lies in healing the split that originates in the very foundation of our lives, our culture, our languages, our thoughts. A massive uprooting of dualistic thinking in the individual and collective unconscious is the beginning of a long struggle, but one that could, in our best hopes, bring us to the end of rape, of violence, of war.[50]

The differing and deferring of différance facilitates such uprooting because it disrupts the hermeticism of the dyadic model and opens it to a social world of reference that forces it beyond itself.[51] According to Richard Terdiman, the truth about the sign becomes its story, "a narration of the unfolding of its meaning which we can no longer conceive as preexisting substance. It must be comprehended as *production*, as determined by its relation to other social series beyond itself."[52] In other words, the movement of différance symbolically resists the preexisting substance of nationalist identity by escalating the formal undecidability of Moses' national identity into a counterdiscourse of hybridity, that is, Moses as the signifier of a new racial and national "mixedness." Once again we glimpse how the strategies of deconstruction can become potent political weapons.

This seems especially ironic at a time when many claim that the use of deconstructive practices leads only to nihilism and reactionary—if not proto-Fascist—politics.[53] Of course, one could not charge Hurston with this accusation since she never characterized her work in terms of différance, and her distrust of the totalizing impulse developed years before Derrida and the discovery of Paul de Man's Nazi collaborationist writings in *Le Soir*. Reflecting on this debacle, Geoffrey Hartmann—a Jewish scholar-critic as well as a close friend of de Man's—writes that in light of the *Le Soir* discovery, his deconstructive turn "appears more and more as a deepening reflection on the rhetoric of totalitarianism. . . . De Man's critique of every tendency to totalize literature or language, to see unity where there is no unity, looks like a belated, but still powerful, act of conscience."[54] In a provocative way, Hurston's efforts to fracture organic identity emerge from the same political crucible—the ethnocentric nationalism whose final solution defied the limits of human evil. Along with the Psalmist, she proclaims to all who will hear: "The boundary lines have fallen for me in pleasant places; surely I have a delightful inheritance" (Ps. 16:6).

7

(ex)Changing (wo)Man

Let me introduce you to Zeno: no, not the philosopher of paradox but the thief, who has stolen both a gold pocket watch from
the world of conventional signs and the answer sheets for the
upcoming graduate record exam. At the moment of our intervention in Donald Barthelme's essay "Not-Knowing," Jacqueline
and Jemima (two Sarah Lawrence seniors who have just failed
the graduate record exam) are instructing Zeno (who has since
returned the purloined letters) in postmodernism:

> Postmodernism, they tell him, has turned its back on the
> world, is not about the world but about its own processes,
> is masturbatory, certainly chilly, excludes readers by design,
> speaks only to the already tenured, or does not speak at all,
> but instead—
> Zeno, to demonstrate that he too knows a thing or too,
> quotes the critic Perry Meisel on semiotics. "Semiotics," he
> says, "is in a position to claim that no phenomenon has any
> ontological status outside its place in the particular infor-
> mation system from which it draws its meaning"—he takes

a large gulp of his Gibson—"and therefore, all language is finally groundless." I am eavesdropping and I am much reassured. This insight is one I can use. Gaston, the [literary] critic who is a guard at the Whitney Museum, is in love with an IRS agent named Madelaine, the very IRS agent, in fact, who is auditing my return for the year 1982. "Madelaine," I say kindly to her over lunch, "semiotics is in a position to claim that no phenomenon has any ontological status outside its place in the particular information system from which it draws its meaning, and therefore, all language is finally groundless, including that of those funny little notices you've been sending me." "Yes," says Madelaine kindly, pulling from her pocket a large gold pocket watch . . . her lovely eyes atwitter, "but some information systems are more enforceable than others."[1]

Between his gulps of Gibson, Zeno describes what might be called the *via dolorosa* of contemporary postmodernism: because of its failure of theory, because of its abstracting, ahistorical discourse with little responsibility toward the real, its semiotic instrument seems doomed to an endlessly repetitive and self-reflexive circulation of meaning.[2] This semiotic navel-gazing also highlights the irony of having Madelaine represent an information system that the IRS guarantees to be more enforceable than others: if real men don't eat quiche, real women don't carry gold pocket watches. Like Zeno, postmodernism has robbed them of public time by metaphorizing them as repressed space.

In the postmodernist construct of "woman," for example—that "other-than-themselves" within Western master narratives which is "almost always a 'space' of some kind (over which the narrative has lost control)"—this repressed space has been coded as feminine, as woman.[3] "Woman" as the nodal point for the postmodern project of reconceptualizing Man, Subject, Truth, History, and Meaning exists neither as a person nor as a thing; rather, as Alice Jardine notes, "she" is a critical horizon toward which this reconceptualizing process tends, a reading effect or woman-in-effect who lacks stability and the permanence of historical identity.

However, "woman's" testing of Western metaphysical boundaries simultaneously *con*tests claims made by biological-historical women. Through "her," postmodernism sets into motion a contradiction that many feminists find very troubling indeed: "To refuse 'woman' or the 'feminine' as cultural and libidinal constructions (as in 'men's femininity') is, ironically, to return to metaphysical— anatomical—definitions of sexual identity. To accept a metaphorization, a semiosis of woman, on the other hand, means risking once again the absence of women as subjects in the struggles of modernity."[4] The terms of this statement discourage feminist theorists from employing for their own ends perhaps the most subversive strategy of postmodernism, that is, putting the terms of a contradiction "under erasure" and into question. This questioning is exactly what this chapter will consider by developing the striking similarity of "woman" within postmodernism to women as commodities within capitalist patriarchy. Both are intimate friends, if not relatives, of the same family roots—the "exchange abstraction," or the particular mode of social interrelationship that evolves in a society based upon commodity exchange.[5]

It seems all too clear that the failure to grasp this familial bond underlies much of the antagonism currently existing between those feminists influenced by deconstruction and other variations of postmodernist theory and those often pejoratively described by the former as "naive realists." In *Intellectual and Manual Labor: A Critique of Epistemology*, Alfred Sohn-Rethel observes that a formal analysis of the commodity holds the key not only to the most incisive critique of Western political economy but also to the historical explanation of the abstract conceptual mode of thinking that has so dominated Anglo-European epistemology.[6] One could make a similar argument concerning the networks of social and discursive exchange engendered in a capitalist society. Through an analysis of women and "woman" as commodities on the market, I hope to provide a framework for bridging the impasse within contemporary feminist discourse, for "on this crucial relation of woman as constituted in representation to women as historical subjects depend at once the development of a feminist critique and the possibility of a materialist, semiotic theory of culture."[7]

Such a project, which I am calling a "materialist-feminist semiotics," implies both a critical and constructive movement. The critical movement insists upon the intersection of ideas and language with the social and historical[8] and tries to bring the idealist construct of "woman" back into relation with its ideological underpinnings. The constructive movement elaborates a theory of signification grounded in the experience of women as they have lived it—without, however, denying the important insight of postmodernism that we only grasp this experience through particular discourses. A materialist-feminist semiotics requires that we not only recognize how micrologies of power keep certain information systems in place while simultaneously suppressing others but also resist the temptation of an unmediated politics of meaning. With this double-edged task in mind, we can now move to the critical phase, or an examination of the social and discursive traffic in women.

THE TRAFFIC IN WOMEN

But I didn't leave all the parts of me; I kept the ground of my own being.
            Gloria Anzaldúa, *Borderlands/La Frontera*

In order to demonstrate the collusion between capitalist patriarchy's exchange of women and postmodernism's exchange of "woman," we need to search for our mothers' gardens—a search that in this case returns us to late nineteenth-century South Africa and to Olive Schreiner, who is perhaps best known for her novel, *The Story of an African Farm*, and her treatise on "sex-parasitism" *Woman and Labor*. However, I want to focus upon a more marginal work of Schreiner's, her unfinished novel *From Man to Man*. As one might imagine from the title, the patriarchal and capitalist traffic in women provides both the narrative and thematic structure of this work. Indeed, it specifically addresses the problem of women as commodities through the lives of two sisters: Rebekah, who becomes an estranged wife, prevented by moral and legal sanctions from loving the only man she regards as an equal; and Bertie, raped and shunned, who dies a prostitute in a cheap Cape Town bordello. The fact that Schreiner links these two tragic fates of women through a sisterly relation textually inscribes her belief that the difference between a legal wife and an illegal prostitute is merely one of degree. Schreiner would emphatically agree with her political sister Emma Goldman that "it is merely a question of degree whether she sells herself to one man, in or out of marriage, or to many men"[9]—both estates are spawned by a society that naturalizes the exchange of women through their institutionalized social and economic inferiority.

Baby Bertie's afflictions begin with the violation of her fifteen-year-old virginity by Percie Lawrie, the young tutor whom her family has lovingly hired to complete her education. However, if we go in search of Bertie's garden, we do not discover the nurturing presence of our foremothers but rather the brutal scene of Bertie's "de-flowering": "Bertie's little wild-flower garden was destroyed. . . . All the plants had been pulled up by the roots and the ground trampled flat."[10] Her agonies come to a climax when she confesses this sexual encounter to her cousin and fiancé, John-Ferdinand. With a poignant appropriateness, the smell of "crushed geraniums" perfumes the air as he realizes that Bertie's "sin" has forever soiled the most "absolutely spotless, Christ-like thing I have known" and ruined her value as a wife—that female commodity exchanged patronymically from father to husband.

John-Ferdinand's perception of a pristine feminine essence contaminated by even the tiniest sexual stain concretely embodies Marx's visual analogy for commodity fetishism: the logic of substitution transforms the social products of labor into objectified commodities just as "the impression made by a thing on the optic nerve is perceived not as a subjective excitation of that nerve but as the objective form of a thing outside the eye. In the act of seeing, of course, light is really transmitted from one thing, the external object, to another thing, the eye. It is a physical relation *between* things" (emphasis added).[11] It is precisely this interrelationship that commodity fetishism denies: like the eye that suppresses its own part in the act of perceiving, commodity fetishism suppresses the origins of the commodity within the social processes of human labor. Thus, it achieves its social synthesis by concealing the true identity of the commodity in the guise of a "thing"—money, for example—which one can carry about in a wallet, hand out to others, and, in turn, receive from others.[12]

In the case of Bertie, the misprision of capitalism construes her sensuous human subjectivity abstractly, perceiving it as an object reduced to a common value to be exchanged against another.[13] Like all women bound by capitalist and patriarchal exchange, Bertie becomes "reduced to some common feature—their current price in gold, or phalluses—and of which they would represent a plus or minus quantity,"[14] and her fate provides eloquent testimony that her primary value resides in a sexual purity quantitatively measured and inexorably required.

Bertie responds to her "sin" by making her commodification explicit and eloping with a wealthy Jewish moneylender who takes her to London and maintains her in luxury as a pampered yet imprisoned mistress. Within the novel, the assigned role of the character known only as "the Jew" serves to locate Bertie's status as a desirable commodity firmly within the capitalist system. The exchange abstraction structures their relationship through the capitalist misprision of "the Jew's" perception from the moment he meets Bertie: she never exists for him as an independent material being but only as a generic replacement who seems to duplicate his long-dead wife. In an intolerable contradiction, however, the anti-Semitism embedded in the cultural stereotype of Jews as moneylenders colludes with the author's own capitalist misprision by connecting the ethnic identity of "the Jew" to Bertie's loss of ontology. Although as a male he might very well participate in the exchange abstraction of women, as a Jew he experiences legal and social ostracism in turn-of-the-century English society. Indeed, displacing the origins of Bertie's growing invisibility onto Christianity's marginalized Other mystifies the structures of capitalist patriarchy, for its most ominous practitioners are not Jews but Anglo-European middle- and upper-class men.

Bertie's walks with Isaac, the retarded son of the Jew's housekeeper, vividly reveal her internalization of the commodity's particular malaise: "They were real houses, with real people; it was not a nightmare; they were all real; it was she and Isaac walking up and down, up and down on the pavement, that were so strange" (*FMM* 357). One way to understand the political stakes of this passage is to examine the exchange abstraction it so unwittingly describes. The capitalist process of exchange requires that its objects remain immutable during all phases of its transactions; exchange not only abstracts the material content from commodities and substitutes contents of purely human significance but also "excludes everything that makes up history. . . . The entire empirical reality of facts, events and description by which one moment and locality of time and space is distinguishable from another is wiped out."[15] In one of the novel's most moving examples of women's pathos, Bertie's startling growth of appetite and her subsequent obesity during her liaison with the Jew function as desperately inadequate attempts to resist this loss of ontology.

The pathology induced by the exchange abstraction dramatically illustrates the absolute timelessness and universality that mark it. As Sohn-Rethel remarks: "There, in the market-place and in shop windows, things stand still. They are under the spell of one activity only: to change owners."[16] Bertie's virtual imprisonment in and bewitchment by the historical vacuum of the Jew's house provides the narrative equivalent of this spell. She is forbidden to leave the house without an escort, to speak with any acquaintances when walking, and to explore the parts of the house concerned with business. Time is erased from her consciousness because its very existence poses a threat to the necessarily ahistorical network of exchange.

In the novel, then, a profoundly hierarchical dualism characterizes Bertie's status. She is structured as a commodity through the opposition of private space to public world, interchange with nature to interchange with society, mind to body, quantity to quality, and ideal to material.[17] The kenosis engendered by the exchange abstraction—the way the commodity empties itself of all sensuous historical content—uncovers the conversion of social configurations structured by exchange into the epistemological forms peculiar to those epochs. In other words, it reveals the invisible tie binding women as social commodities to "woman" as discursive commodity. While the opposition of quantity to quality certainly marks Bertie's tragic exchange from man to man, I would contend that the second—the separation of natural and social interaction—is the distinguishing characteristic of the postmodernist "woman."

Now the phenomenon of the social body is the effect not of a consensus but of the materiality of power operating on the very bodies
of individuals.

Michel Foucault, "Body/Power"

"Woman," as the saying goes, has become a metaphor without
brakes.[18] Jacques Derrida diagnoses the mechanical failure that
leads to "woman" careening out of control down the slippery slope
of postmodernism when he comments that her "spacing designates
nothing, nothing, that is, no presence. . . . It is . . . a displacement
that indicates an irreducible alterity."[19] To use a pregnant metaphor, it is not just that "woman's" production/reproduction of
human materiality is ectopic, or misplaced; rather, it is "atopic"
because it lacks a place entirely. Consequently, historical and biological women who have accepted personal space as an important
source of political truth (for example, "the personal is political")
now find themselves denigrated as "naive romanticists" (Kristeva)
or "reactive specularists" (Derrida) who perversely refuse to acknowledge "the demise of [feminist] experience" (Jardine). A
woman like this only aspires "to be like a [phallogocentric] man . . .
and lays claim—just as much as he—to truth."[20]

The image that most frequently conjures this atopia is that of
"woman" the ballerina. In his interview with Christie McDonald,
for example, Derrida develops the image of the female dancer into
an elaborate articulation of postmodernism's relation to the feminist movement. Yet, the choreography that he creates for "her"
curiously reenacts the ballet of the Red Shoes. Like the heroine
of the story, once "woman" puts on her deconstructive slippers,
she can never stop dancing; her "indefinitely pivoting pirouettes
mark the spots of what can never be mediated, mastered, sub-
lated or dialecticized."[21] These indeterminate pirouettes further
signify that "woman" no longer contains an identifiable content.
"She" performs the characteristic movement of deconstruction
by inhabiting such binary oppositions as nature/culture or man/

(ex)Changing (wo)Man

woman, resisting and disorganizing them without ever becoming a positive third term. In this way, remarks Shosanna Felman in "Re-reading Femininity," "femininity as real otherness . . . is uncanny in that it is not the opposite of masculinity, but *that which subverts the very opposition of masculinity and femininity*."[22] What this alleged subversion of masculine and feminine opposites conceals, however, is that the disruption of its dualism occurs only by installing a new and perhaps even more dangerous opposition—that between the postmodern "woman" and bio-historical women; between the ethereal ballerina of deconstruction and the flat-footed ethicist of feminism.

The textualism of Jacques Derrida and Julia Kristeva defines "woman" as a purely social and linguistic value that radically opposes any positive "natural" value. This opposition clearly characterizes Kristeva's now famous assertion that "a feminist practice can only be negative, at odds with what already exists. . . . In 'woman' I see something that cannot be represented, something that is not said."[23] In "woman" *I* see some "thing" whose status as a commodity has been covered over in the hegemonic exchanges of postmodern discourse. I would argue that the postmodern construction of "woman" represents the ultimate development of the exchange abstraction, for in order to glue Western discourse together, "she" must be marked by a homogeneity (one might appropriate the title of Robert Musil's *roman à thèse* and name the text of postmodernism *The "Woman" without Qualities*) that is emptied of all sensuous and often contradictory historical content. "Woman" belies the contention that "she" represents a new rhetorical space inseparable from the most radical moments of contemporary thought,[24] for postmodernism still trades upon a phallic symbolic economy. It has made its theoretical (and in some cases, literal) fortune by metamorphosing "woman" into a discursive Orphan Annie whose dependence on Daddy's postmodern Warbucks endows her only with invisibility, negativity, and difference.

In his comparison of the exchange of women within culture and the execution of a game of chess, Claude Lévi-Strauss provides us with a way of considering the relationship between women and "woman" as mutually implicated rather than opposed: "The skillful game of exchange (in which there is very often no more real transfer than in a game of chess, in which the players do not give each other the pieces they alternately move forward on the chessboard but merely seek to provoke a counter-move), consists in a complex totality of conscious or unconscious manoeuvre in order to gain security and to guard oneself against risks brought about by alliances and rivalries."[25] Since a game is socially constructed, the analogy of exchange and chess puts the oppression of women in cultural rather than biological terms and suggests that its political economy is also a vehicle for realities of a different order, such as power, influence, and status.

The irony here is that Lévi-Strauss describes the political stakes of this game yet fails to recognize either the gendered nature of the rules or the oppression that the game's moves and countermoves perpetuate. In fact, one could read Alice's exclamation in *Through the Looking Glass* as a feminist gloss upon just this point: " 'I declare it's marked out just like a large chess-board!' Alice said at last. 'There ought to be some men moving about somewhere— and so there are!' she added in a tone of delight. . . . 'It's a great huge game of chess that's being played—all over the world.' "[26] Alice intuits that the game of chess/exchange moves forward as a sexual war whose "Rules of Battle" (the chivalric code of the White and Red Knights) legitimate the appropriation of women in order to protect patriarchal power. Like Alice—the White's pawn captured by the Red Knight—women lament their imprisonment in the nets of exchange; unlike Alice, however, they realize that becoming a Queen, or the chess piece with the most power on the board, remains only a fantasy for a children's tale.

Lévi-Strauss implicitly affirms the accuracy of Alice's claim when he notes that the exchange of women possesses an intrinsically positive social value, for it provides the means of binding men together and of superimposing upon the "natural" links of kinship the artificial links of alliance governed by rule.[27] This observation, combined with his portrayal of exchange as a vehicle for realities of a different order, firmly embeds it within a semiosis of patriarchal culture, or that process by which a culture produces signs and/or attributes meaning to them.[28] If a sign is "*everything* that, on the grounds of a previously established social convention, can be taken as *something standing for something else*,"[29] then women who are exchanged become signs, for only a woman's symbolic value differentiates her from all other women within the same system. Or, according to Umberto Eco in *A Theory of Semiotics*, the moment a woman becomes a "wife" she is no longer merely a physical body but a sign that conjures a whole system of social constraint and obligation.[30]

Obviously not anticipating the ahistoricizing thrusts of postmodernism, Lévi-Strauss contends that "woman could never become just a sign and nothing more, since even in a man's world she is still a person, and since in so far as she is defined as a sign she must be recognized as a generator of signs."[31] According to Lévi-Strauss's analysis, women retain both a positive economic value as "wife" (a generator of signs) and a negative communicative value as "sign" within the exchanges of kinship. Postmodernism, however, splits this feminine ambivalence apart: its production of meaningful speech by exchanging one set of words for another denies not only that "woman" is a generator of signs but also that she possesses an embodied voice. This network of exchange posits women as social signs and "woman" as discursive sign in terms of moments separated by degree rather than substance within the larger semiosis of patriarchal culture.

A materialist-feminist analysis must reject any theory of signification based upon the kenotic epistemology of the exchange abstraction since it imposes false dichotomies upon the way women experience reality. A genuinely feminist semiotics can emerge only from the historicity of women's lives *as they have lived them* and must root imagination and the production of ideas solidly within the conditions of their material experience as women and workers. In the second, or constructive, phase of a materialist-feminist semiotics, "their [women/commodities] situation of specific exploitation in exchange operations—sexual exchange, and economic, social and cultural exchanges in general—might well lead them to offer a new critique of political economy. A critique that would no longer avoid that of discourse, and more generally of the symbolic system, in which it is realized. Which would lead to interpreting in a different way the impact of symbolic social labor in the analysis of relations of production."[32] In this new materialist-feminist semiotics, the perception of how humans make meaning would not depend upon exchanging woman but rather upon changing man.

> Let us do what no idealist has done: seek unrealities. . . . We shall find them, I believe, in the dialectic of Zeno. . . . We (the undivided divinity operating within us) have dreamt the world. We have dreamt of it as firm, mysterious, visible, ubiquitous in space and durable in time; but in its architecture we have allowed tenuous and eternal crevices of unreason which tell us it is false.
>
> Jorge Luis Borges, "Avatars of the Tortoise"

At this point, we need to return to Zeno—no, not the thief (one would hope that by now we have forced him to return the gold pocket watch to the world of conventional signs), but Zeno the philosopher of paradox who said you can't get there from here. His most famous paradox, of course, is the story of Achilles, the tortoise, and the riddles of infinite divisibility—several close readings of which awakened a desperate longing for the strong black coffee that would alert me to what I had obviously been missing. While I made the coffee, my spouse, himself a philosopher (but who takes no responsibility for Zeno), tried to illuminate the nuances of infinite divisibility, but to very little profit indeed. "Of course," I pronounced, my commonsense self briskly taking hold of the situation, "even *I* could beat the tortoise—it seems perfectly obvious!" This literal instance of philosophy in the kitchen ironically dramatizes the danger of feminist discourse proclaiming its own "Of course!" and taking purely affirmative action without questioning the structures that make such unproblematic movement conceivable. Once again, Olive Schreiner points the way for us in her construction of a feminist standpoint that is also allegorical.

In *Woman and Labor*, Schreiner declares that woman as a material being with an ontologically positive status "has something radically distinct to contribute to the sum-total of human knowledge, and her activity is of importance, not merely individually, but collectively, and as a class."[33] The contention that women's experience differs systematically from men's raises the question of both gender as a worldview-structuring experience and the possibility of a feminist standpoint. As a morally preferable grounding for interpreting natural and social life, a feminist standpoint argues that women's lives—like those of Marx's proletariat—grant them a privileged perspective on the processes of male supremacy: because of their greater immersion in the relational world of the family and the concrete tasks of subsistence labor, women's material experience corrects the partially perverse understandings that originate in the dominating position of men. This enables them to develop a powerful criticism of the phallocratic institutions and dualistic epistemology that characterize the networks of exchange in its capitalist and patriarchal form.[34] This characterization of a feminist standpoint seems very close to what Schreiner herself envisioned in her remark that "it is perhaps woman, by reason of those very sexual conditions which in the past have crushed and trammelled her, who is bound to lead the way, and man to follow."[35]

In *Money, Sex, and Power: Toward a Feminist Historical Materialism*, Nancy Hartsock calls such a standpoint "feminist" rather than "female" because of its achieved character in discerning and amplifying the liberatory possibilities contained in feminine experience. It seems especially interesting in this context that Schreiner begins *From Man to Man* with a narrative of birth—a story of the reproduction of kinship relations—which is framed by Rebekah's efforts to liberate her newly born sister from the tyrannies of exchange. A five-year-old Rebekah, "her tiny features curiously set with the firmness of a woman's," climbs into the room where they have laid the infant, drapes it in her best fur-trimmed cloak, and ritually bedecks it with gifts from her beloved treasure box. In an extremely suggestive parallel, the function of these gifts closely duplicates Lévi-Strauss's analysis of the cross-cultural function of gifts at a potlatch: they publicly establish one's claim to a title or prerogative and officially announce a change of status. Rebekah's childish activities and her ferocious assertion that "*this one* is mine!" could likewise signify a public announcement of her prerogative to change her sister's status from that of commodified object to participant in a more woman-centered order of meaning.[36]

The fact that immediately after this episode Rebekah dreams what she calls a "self-to-self" story corroborates this interpretation, for the meaning of self-to-self stories depends upon the free interchange of subject-selves rather than the oppressive exchange of object-women. Rebekah's dreamself, who becomes a mother by discovering a baby daughter inside a mimosa pod, embodies Schreiner's belief that women's "distinct psychic attitude" germinates in their lived experience of maternity.[37] Because gestation involves the most extreme suspension of the bodily distinction between inner and outer, it questions the relationship between self and other, or subject and object, as one of confrontation and opposition; instead, maternity constitutes them as a continuity in difference.[38] Rebekah's ethic of mothering likewise displaces the dualism of exchange ("My baby, I shall never call *you* 'a strange child' ") and literally leads the way for men to follow by embarking upon a dream journey structured by a feminist standpoint.

In this story within a story, the protagonist—a young girl much like Rebekah herself—takes a walk through the African bush. A series of encounters with various wild animals demonstrates her connected and relational perspective, for in each case, she embraces what society has traditionally feared as other and opens herself to significant engagement with it: she plays, for example, with the newborn offspring of a puff adder, one of the world's most poisonous snakes, and promises to bring them milk when she can find some. For the girl in Rebekah's story, as for a feminist standpoint, "the supreme moment to me is not when I kill or conquer a living thing, but that moment when its eye and mine meet and a line of connection is formed between me and the life that is in it."[39]

However, as Hartsock herself notes yet ultimately disregards, the danger of adopting a feminist standpoint as the locus of meaning is the possibility of rendering the experience of women of color and lesbians invisible. Further, a standpoint based upon maternity seems dangerously close to a form of biological determinism, for it assumes that all women bear children and thus excludes the perspective of women, whether lesbian or heterosexual, who choose not to have children. In this respect, feminists would do well to note that at this point in the novel, Rebekah's participation in motherhood is metaphorical rather than biological.

Just as this standpoint presupposes that all women are mothers, it also houses their families by constructing a feminist version of Levittown: regardless of who lives in them, all the houses are the same. This insistence upon a homogenous blueprint for feminism and the refusal to question ourselves as we traverse the heterogeneous categories of race, class, and sex abjure "the need for a new sense of political community which gives up desire for the kind of home where the suppression of positive differences underwrites familial identity."[40] The "family of man" always passed on its patronymy by suppressing the existence of women; the family of woman cannot afford to pass on its "matronymy" through the same marginalizing dynamic.

Schreiner provides us with a provocative model for thinking through these issues of homogeneity and universality by imbuing her feminist standpoint with an allegorical vision. In an October 1909 letter to Mrs. Frances Smith, she describes "The Prelude," the opening sequence of *Man*, as "a kind of allegory, of the life of the woman in the book! It's one of the strangest things I know of. My mind must have been working at it *unconsciously*, though I know nothing of it—otherwise how did it come?"[41] In fact, Schreiner has instinctively created "a kind of allegory" about women's lives that is also a metanarrative—a narrative about the way women weave and communicate their own narratives—which disentangles them from the exchange abstraction and leads them to a more woman-centered discursive economy. Schreiner's construing of this metanarrative as allegorical gives it a startling relevance in light of the critical travails of contemporary feminism: it not only grounds itself in the matter of women's existence as they have lived it but also negotiates the contradiction between a radical politics of identity and a postmodernist skepticism, an unqualified opposition and purely affirmative action, which threatens feminism from within. Teresa de Lauretis persuasively argues that the task of feminist theory is "to negotiate that contradiction, to keep it going . . . to resist the pressure of . . . the production of a fixed self/image . . . and to insist instead on the production of contradictory points of identification, an elsewhere of vision."[42] It is precisely this elsewhere of vision that Schreiner's metanarrative creates through its affirmation of the allegorical perspective.

In her communication with Smith, Schreiner asks: "When you read that little 'Prelude' to my book I showed you the other day, did you think it was a *made-up thing*, like an allegory, or did you think it was real *about myself*?"[43] It is precisely this "made-up" quality that constitutes the traditional distinction between allegory and symbol and that explains why postmodernism has adopted allegory as the trope of preference in its critique of the Western classical tradition. Because it imposes an arbitrary meaning upon narrative, "allegory prompts us to say of any cultural description not 'this represents, or symbolizes, that' but rather, 'this is a (morally charged) *story* about that.' "[44] Allegory not only exposes the ideological underpinnings of discourse but also problematizes a symbolic metaphysics of presence, or in the case of a feminist standpoint, a radical politics of identity.

A semiotic practice based upon the symbol seeks to reinstate the myth of unmediated meaning by arguing that the relationship between the symbolized and the symbol emerges spontaneously from their identification with, and participation in, the substance of the other.[45] Julia Kristeva illuminates the importance of this statement for feminist theory when she describes the semantics of the symbol in terms of restriction: "In its horizontal dimension (the articulation of signifying units in relation to one another) the function of the symbol is one of escaping the paradox; one might say that the symbol is horizontally *anti-paradoxical*: within its 'logic' two opposing units are exclusive."[46] Since identity and opposition are two sides of the same coin, both deny contradiction. This process seems very much akin to the "horizontal violence," or what Monique Wittig has called "the material oppression of individuals by discourses,"[47] which often vitiates feminist theorizing of women's experience. In its own escaping of paradox, a feminist standpoint conflates all women's experience into a unitary (white, middle-class) identity, thus excluding that which is different.

Unlike the symbol, allegory implies a much more discontinuous relation between signifier and signified, since an extraneous principle rather than some natural identification determines how and when their connection becomes articulated.[48] Allegory creates meaning metonymically by temporally displacing reference from one sign to the next; in other words, its always mobile construction of meaning resists a representational truth, or the attempt to find an invariant signified for the narrative that can then be placed before the reader for acceptance or rejection.[49] Likewise, an allegorical feminism resists not only a representational view of women's truth but also the unified Cartesian subject that such a view presupposes. Allegory highlights the irrevocably relational nature of feminist identity and the negations upon which the assumption of a singular, fixed, and essential self is based.[50]

However, since an allegory also forms a coherent narrative, one could say that it approximates the "continuity in difference" that characterizes a feminist standpoint germinating from the lived or imagined experience of pregnancy, for both necessitate a positive disintegration of the unitary self into a more processual and multiplicitous entity. In his essay "On Ethnographic Allegory," James Clifford comments that a scientific ethnography normally establishes a privileged register it identifies as "theory," "interpretation," or "explanation," which imparts an authoritative meaning to the rest of the narrative. "But," he continues, "once *all* meaningful levels in a text, including theories and interpretation, are recognized as allegorical, it becomes difficult to view one of them as privileged, accounting for the rest. Once this anchor is dislodged, the staging and valuing of multiple allegorical registers, or 'voices,' becomes an important area of concern."[51] Only when the white woman's feminist movement recognizes its own voice as allegorical will it be able to repudiate its race and class—privileged—and therefore distorted—accounting for *all* women. Only then will it replace a univocal feminine voice with one that is plurivocal, for the allegorical mode connects women yet requires them to speak in many tongues.

I should hasten to add that this recognition of multiple allegorical registers in the ethnography of women's experience is not the radical skepticism of a feminist postmodernism but rather an articulation of postmodernism's most powerful insights in a different voice. Feminist theory must accomplish an extremely difficult task, for it must discern the experiential connections that surely exist among women and simultaneously refuse to privilege any particular connection as that which subsumes the rest. In this context, Schreiner once again bequeaths us a prophetic image through which to construct an elsewhere of vision that will lead us into a truly liberating feminist future. Surrounded by her racially mixed children in the country of apartheid, Rebekah dreams of a new material space for women: " 'Out there in my garden,' she said softly, 'there are flowers of all kinds growing—tall queen-lilies and roses and pinks and violets and little brown ranunculuses— and I love them all. But if the tall queen-lilies were to say, "We must reign here alone, all the others must die to give place to us," I do not know, but I think I might say, "Is it not perhaps then best *you* should go?" ' " (*FMM* 418).

We as feminists must attend to a search for our mothers' gardens, which is both grammatically and existentially plural. The gardens that engender feminist standpoints do indeed exist, but we as gardeners-interpreters must recognize the diversity of their ecologies and of the ways they cultivate meaning. The allegorical imagination of Olive Schreiner is an important tool in implementing just such a materialist-feminist semiosis of culture. Her multiplicitous cultivating has primed the ground for this contemporary generation of women, and we ignore it at the peril of our own perspectival sterility and the theoretical equivalent of ecological disaster.

On Women's "Experience"

Postscript

The meaning of experience is perhaps the most crucial site of political struggle over meaning.
  Chris Weedon, Feminist Practice and Poststructuralist Theory

At the 1990 National Women's Studies Association Conference in Akron, Ohio, the Women of Color Caucus and its various supporters walked out of the meeting to dramatize allegations of racism within the association and, ultimately, to form their own Women of Color Association. The words of these women (published in the February 1991 *Women's Review of Books*) are especially eloquent in presenting women's "experience" as a contested site within feminism:

> [Sondra O'Neale:] We no longer have to feel bound by any hierarchical definition of feminism. . . . Each of us is free to define ourselves and our feminist philosophies as represented by our own historical frameworks and by the urgencies within our respective communities.

[Maria Lugones:] It is time to form deep coalitions by becoming listeners and speakers of each other's voices without looking for a simple but complex unity, or, maybe better expressed, by looking for solidarity in multiplicity. We have to become self-critical as we learn enough about each other to become critical of each other.

Linda Gardiner, the editor of *Women's Review of Books*, comments that, while women of color organized their own autonomous organization, the women still "committed to the survival of NWSA are asking themselves what lessons for the future are to be learned from these events." The lesson that dominant feminism desperately needs to learn is precisely how it can form the "deep coalitions" or "solidarity in multiplicity" so necessary to its survival as a revolutionary movement.

Perhaps the reason why this question has become so fraught with danger, and why it seems so difficult to answer, is feminism's reluctance to recognize women's "experience" as a category that mediates between the raw material data of a life and its cultural construction as subjectivity. As such, one must interpret "experience" in semiotic or, in the terms of chapter 7, allegorical terms. If semiosis implies the ability to recognize given phenomena as part of a world that makes good sense, then "we judge the items of our experience not in and of themselves, as unique phenomena in experience, but instead in relation to some other structure of meaning."[1] As Teresa de Lauretis notes, "experience" signifies that complex of habits resulting from the semiotic interaction of our inner and outer worlds and the continuous engagement of a subject with social reality.[2] For each person, then, "experience" is an ongoing construction, "not a fixed point of departure or arrival from which one then interacts with the world."[3] Therefore, women cannot appeal to some transparently universal ground of being but rather must negotiate the meaning of feminine identity in relation to structures of language, sex, race, class, age, physical ability, nationality, religion, and so forth.

No era more clearly demonstrates the need for this semiotic negotiation than nineteenth-century British colonialism, since its contradictions shatter the glass house that feminism has constructed from a univocal gender identity. In the context of colonialism, for example, women's shared experience of reproduction becomes much more problematic as the basis for a feminist standpoint (see chapter 7). Would we really want to argue that "Mrs. Anna's" experience of motherhood in an imperialist and cosmopolitan European framework also speaks for the colonized tribal experience of an Aboriginal woman? Would we want to argue that women who do not bear children negotiate the meaning of reproduction in the same way as women who do? One could only answer "yes" to these queries by regarding reproduction as a purely biological, that is, naturalized, function that is separable from any human consciousness of reproduction. Yet this appeal to an unmediated materialism is precisely how many feminists define women's "experience."

In *The Politics of Reproduction*, former midwife and current feminist theorist Mary O'Brien argues the importance of Marx's insight that all human interaction with nature involves a *process*, which is "dialectical, an active series of negations and mediations."[4] Human reproduction thus becomes inseparable from human consciousness of reproduction. While women do share the same involuntary biology of reproduction in menstruation and ovulation, they do not share the same consciousness of that biology. As O'Brien observes, women's "reproductive consciousness," that is, the knowledge of themselves as potential reproducers, is culturally transmitted[5] and must be negotiated through the semioticity of all meaningful experience.

Like the feminist history that Katie King describes in her essay "Producing Sex, Theory, and Culture: Gay/Straight Remappings in Contemporary Feminism," what is taken for women's "experience" are some privileged and published accounts of it, which feminism has naturalized. And, like the multiple sexual histories that King has used to riddle feminist history with contradictions,[6] colonialism problematizes the category of women's "experience" by its production of gender as a contested discursive field. The materialist-feminist semiotics that I articulated in chapter 7 only begins the task of unraveling and then reweaving the material and symbolic threads constituting the textures and texts of women's lives. Unless and until women understand the asymmetrical patterns of their "experience," it will be difficult for us to transcend our blindnesses and become "listeners and speakers of each other's voices."

Jane Eyre, Mrs. Anna Leonowens, Mrs. Aeneas Gunn, Adela Quested, Bertha Mason, Tuptim, Bett-Bett, "India"—the imbricated narratives of these historical and fictional characters constitute a new story field for feminism in which "the stories can only be generated, told, and read in relation to each other."[7] Such a story field denies the privileging of any one plot (or gender identity) for women's lives in its affirmation of stor*ies* (and gender*s*); it also demands that each story negotiate its position in relation to all other stories included within the field, which in turn must recalculate their own positions. This model aptly describes that "solidarity in multiplicity" so necessary to overcoming the Miranda Complex and, perhaps, provides the enabling conditions for feminism to complete its journey to a postcolonial liberation.

Notes

INTRODUCTION

1. Rich, "Disloyal to Civilization," 299.
2. Pasolini, *Heretical Empiricism*, 87.
3. Przybylowicz, "Feminist Cultural Criticism," 260.
4. Mohanty, "Under Western Eyes," 53.
5. Ibid., 52.
6. Meese, *(Ex)tensions*, 23.
7. Weedon, *Feminist Practice*, 22.
8. Rowbotham, *Women, Resistance, and Revolution*, 201.
9. Donovan, "Towards a Women's Poetics," 100.
10. French, *Beyond Power*, 130 (hereafter cited in text as *BP*).
11. Bhabha, "Articulating the Archaic," 207.
12. Ibid.
13. Barrett, *Women's Oppression Today* (1988), xi.
14. Memmi, *The Colonizer and the Colonized*, xiii–xiv.
15. Barrett, *Women's Oppression Today* (1988), xii.
16. Weedon, *Feminist Practice*, 27.
17. Sedgwick, *Between Men*, 1.

18. Ibid., 198.

19. Castoriadis, *Imaginary Institution*, 148.

20. Ibid.

21. Jayawardena, *Feminism and Nationalism*, 3.

22. Nyerere, *Freedom and Socialism*, 26–32, as cited in Horace B. Davis, *Toward a Marxist Theory of Nationalism* (New York: Monthly Review Press, 1978), 54–55.

23. Woolf, *Three Guineas* (hereafter cited in text as *TG*).

24. Spivak, *Post-Colonial Critic*, 9.

CHAPTER ONE

1. Ellison, *Invisible Man*, 458 (hereafter cited in text as *IM*).

2. Gilbert and Gubar, *Madwoman in the Attic*, xi (hereafter cited in text as *MA*).

3. Spivak, "Three Women's Texts," 245 (hereafter cited in text as TWT).

4. Spivak, *In Other Worlds*, 209.

5. Baker, "Caliban's Triple Play," 190.

6. Bulhan, *Frantz Fanon*, 189.

7. Feral, "The Powers of Difference," 89.

8. Allen, *Lesbian Philosophy*, 49 (hereafter cited in text as *LP*).

9. Baker, "Caliban's Triple Play," 193.

10. Gates, "The Blackness of Blackness," 287.

11. Teish, *Jambalaya*, 112.

12. Hurston, *Mules and Men*, 193.

13. Teish, "Women's Spirituality," 342.

14. Hurston, *Mules and Men*, 221.

15. Ibid., 231.

16. Fanon, *Black Skin, White Masks*, 217.

17. Smith, Introduction, xxxii.

18. Ogunyemi, "Womanism," 64.

19. Chodorow, *The Reproduction of Mothering*, 166–67.

20. Johnston, "Feminist Film Practice," 323.

21. Brontë, *Jane Eyre*, 31–32 (hereafter cited in text as *JE*).

22. Monaco, *How to Read a Film*, 164.

23. Pudovkin, "On Editing," 87.

24. Silverman, *The Subject of Semiotics*, 205.

25. Ibid., 232.

26. Ibid., 130.

27. Kuhn, *Women's Pictures*, 53.

28. As cited in Silverman, *The Subject of Semiotics*, 233.

29. Ibid.

30. Mulvey, "Visual Pleasure," 809.

31. Kuhn, *Women's Pictures*, 61.

32. Belsey, *Critical Practice*, 75.

33. Ibid., 76.

34. Chesler, *Women and Madness*, 48.

35. Ibid., 49.

36. Ibid.

37. Bulhan, *Frantz Fanon*, 122.

38. Ibid.

CHAPTER TWO

1. French, *The Women's Room*, 7 (hereafter cited in text as *WR*).

2. De Lauretis, *Technologies of Gender*, 1 (hereafter cited in text as *TOG*).

3. Frye, "Separatism and Power," 103.

4. Although Americans have been taught to call Siam "Thailand," the latter is actually a mongrel term introduced in 1939 by Luang Phibunsongskhram, a right-wing nationalist. Before the progressive Prime Minister Pridi Phanomyong was deposed in the 1947 coup, he had restored the country's traditional name of "Siam," thus stressing the rights of minorities as well as of the ethnic Thai. For us to recognize Thailand instead of Siam seems a definite political ambiguity. See Alexander Cockburn, "Beat the Devil," *Nation*, 5 September 1987, 186.

5. Doyle, *Empires*, 51.

6. Shepard, "King Yul," C1.

7. Woolf, *A Room of One's Own*, 24.

8. Landon, *Anna and the King of Siam*, 31 (hereafter cited in text as *AK*). In fact, Landon's "novel" is in many places a word-for-word recounting of Mrs. Leonowens's several diaries.

9. Lehman, "The King and I," screenplay, 22 (hereafter cited in text as KI).

10. Bresson, *Notes on the Cinematographer*, 12.

11. Kaplan, *Women and Film*, 15.

12. For critical evaluations of Mulvey, see especially Kuhn, *Women's Pictures*, 60–62; Gaylyn Studlar's response to Miriam Hansen in *Cinema Journal* 26 (1987): 51–53; de Lauretis, *Technologies of Gender*, 115–24; and Jane Gaines, "White Privilege and Looking Relations—Race and

Gender in Feminist Film Theory," and Manthia Diawara, "Black Spectatorship—Problems of Identification and Resistance," both in *Screen* 29 (1988): 12–27, 66–79. For a sympathetic account of Mulvey, see Silverman, *The Acoustic Mirror*, 29–32. Mulvey has herself reevaluated the original argument in "Visual Pleasure."

13. Mulvey, "Visual Pleasure," 809.

14. Ibid.

15. Margaret Landon notes that the American Francis D. Cobb introduced Anna to Emerson and Stowe while she and her husband were stationed in India. It was through Cobb and her own readings that she became committed to the abolitionist cause.

16. Tompkins, "Sentimental Power," 83 (hereafter cited in text as SP).

17. Stowe, *Uncle Tom's Cabin*, 215 (hereafter cited in text as *UTC*). This edition reproduces the first-edition text as established by Kenneth S. Lynn, editor of the Belknap Press edition published by Harvard University Press in 1962.

18. For more detailed discussions of black women's resistance to slavery, see Davis, *Women, Race, and Class*; Elizabeth Fox-Genovese, "Strategies and Forms of Resistance: Focus on Slave Women in the United States," in *In Resistance: Studies in African, Caribbean, and Afro-American History*, edited by Gary Y. Okihiro (Amherst: University of Massachusetts Press, 1986); and Deborah Gray White, *Ar'n't I a Woman?: Female Slaves in the Plantation South* (London: W. W. Norton and Company, 1985), chap. 2.

19. De Certeau, *Heterologies*, xiii.

20. Davis, *Women, Race, and Class*, 17.

21. Douglass, *Life and Writings*, 2:226.

22. Leonowens, *English Governess*, 20 (hereafter cited in text as *EG*).

23. Ahmed, "Western Ethnocentrism," 526.

24. Leonowens, *Siamese Harem Life*, 11 (hereafter cited in text as *SHL*). This work was originally published in 1873 under the title *The Romance of the Harem*.

25. Ahmed, "Western Ethnocentrism," 528.

26. Ibid.

27. Silverman, "Histoire d'O," 326.

28. Freire, *Pedagogy of the Oppressed*, 31.

29. Ibid., 39.

30. Goontilake, *Crippled Minds*, 91.

31. Feuer, *The Hollywood Musical*, 26.

32. Ibid., 27–28.

33. Ibid., 27.

34. Alloula, *The Colonial Harem*, 38.

35. Cesaire, *Discourse on Colonialism*, 11.

36. Laclau and Mouffe, *Hegemony and Socialist Strategy*, 104.

CHAPTER THREE

1. Stam and Spence, "Colonialism, Racism, and Representation," 635 (hereafter cited in text as CRR).

2. Showalter, "Critical Cross-Dressing," 132.

3. Showalter, "Toward a Feminist Poetics," 128.

4. Holly, "Consciousness and Authenticity," 41.

5. Showalter, "Feminist Criticism in the Wilderness," 266.

6. Todd, *Feminist Literary History*, 75.

7. McDowell, "New Directions," 195.

8. Link and Link-Heer, Foreword, xi. The most obvious example is the Marxist sociology of content approach exemplified by Lucien Goldmann.

9. Ibid.

10. Derrida, "The Double Session," 202.

11. Garner, *The Grafter's Handbook*, 39 (hereafter cited in text as *GH*).

12. *Reader's Digest Illustrated Guide*, 432.

13. Culler, *On Deconstruction*, 135.

14. Link and Link-Heer, Foreword, xiv.

15. Tompkins, *Reader-Response Criticism*, xi.

16. Eagleton, *Ideology*, 6.

17. Ibid., 5.

18. Ibid., 11.

19. Eco, *Role of the Reader*, 22.

20. Gunn, *The Little Black Princess*, 158.

21. Broome, *Aboriginal Australians*, 135.

22. Ibid., 133.

23. Cros, *Sociocriticism*, 50.

24. Terdiman, *Discourse/Counter-Discourse*, 18.

CHAPTER FOUR

1. Memmi, *The Colonizer and the Colonized*, 37 (hereafter cited in text as CC).

2. Spivak, *In Other Worlds*, 179.

3. Moorehead, Foreword, ix.

4. Bates, *The Passing of the Aborigines*, 24 (hereafter cited in text as *PA*).

5. Galeano, *Memory of Fire*, 4.

6. Kristeva, *Language, the Unknown*, 11.

7. Foucault, *History of Sexuality*, 102.

8. Etienne and Leacock, *Women and Colonization*, 18.

9. Ibid.

10. Marx, *Capital*, 1:916.

11. Callinicos, *Marxism and Philosophy*, 151.

12. Gramsci, *Cultural Writings*, 382.

13. Barrie, *Peter Pan* (hereafter cited in text as *PP*). While the novel *Peter Pan* was not published until 1911, the character of Peter first appeared in Barrie's 1902 tale, *The Little White Band*, followed by the play *Peter Pan* two years later.

14. Ricoeur, "Hermeneutical Function," 140.

15. Callinicos, *Marxism and Philosophy*, 147.

16. Fowler, *Literature as Social Discourse*, 94. For an excellent discussion of discourse and the meanings it has accrued within contemporary critical debates, see *A Dictionary of Modern Critical Terms*, rev. ed., edited by Roger Fowler (London: Routledge and Kegan Paul, 1987), 62–66.

17. *Ethnic Notions*, documentary.

18. Barthes, *The Semiotic Challenge*, 58.

19. Ibid., 59.

20. Eco, *A Theory of Semiotics*, 293. The general semiotic analysis is Eco's, but the constructed enthymeme and particular interpretation of the abortion question are my own.

21. Barrett, *Women's Oppression Today* (1980), 111.

22. Laclau and Mouffe, *Hegemony and Socialist Strategy*, 113.

23. MacCabe, "On Discourse," 91.

24. Laclau and Mouffe, *Hegemony and Socialist Strategy*, 113–14.

25. Callinicos, *Marxism and Philosophy*, 153.

26. Dunbar, *J. M. Barrie*, 307.

27. Laclau and Mouffe, *Hegemony and Socialist Strategy*, 110.

28. Ibid.

29. Ibid., 109.

30. Doyle, *Empires*, 130.

31. Ibid., 236.

32. Held, *Introduction to Critical Theory*, 343.

33. Habermas, *Philosophical Discourse*, 322.

34. Barthes, *The Semiotic Challenge*, 267.

35. Gunn, *We of the Never-Never*, 1 (hereafter cited in text as *WNN*).

36. Habermas, *Knowledge and Human Interests*, 223–24.

37. Silverman, "Histoire d'O," 326–27.

38. Silverman and Torode, *The Material Word*, 343.

39. Foucault, "Discourse on Language," 225.

40. Silverman and Torode, *The Material Word*, 342.

41. Habermas, *Philosophical Discourse*, 317.

42. Silverman, "Histoire d'O," 324.

43. Freud, "On Narcissism," 69.

44. Silverman, "Histoire d'O," 325.

45. Ibid., 324.

CHAPTER FIVE

1. Price, "Images of Empire," 32.

2. Ibid.

3. Said, "Through Gringo Eyes," 71.

4. As cited in Price, "Images of Empire," 32.

5. I have adapted Teresa de Lauretis's definition of signifying "practice" to the processes of colonialism. See de Lauretis, *Alice Doesn't*, 37.

6. Bourdieu, *Theory of Practice*, 183–84.

7. See, for example, Spivak, *Post-Colonial Critic*, 39, and Ashis Nandy, *The Intimate Enemy: Loss and Recovery of Self under Colonialism* (Bombay: Oxford University Press, 1983).

8. Bersani, *A Future for Astyanax*, 7.

9. Said, *Orientalism*, 12.

10. Heath, *Questions of Cinema*, 12.

11. Bearce, *British Attitudes towards India*, 104.

12. Ibid., 107.

13. Ibid., 108.

14. Ibid.

15. Mitchell, *Women*, 242.

16. Ibid., 243.

17. As cited in Bhabha, "Articulating the Archaic," 204.

18. Silverman, *The Subject of Semiotics*, 115.

19. Heath, *Questions of Cinema*, 31.

20. Coward, *Female Desires*, 75.

21. Althusser, *For Marx*, 212.

22. Silverman, *The Subject of Semiotics*, 120.

23. Forster, *A Passage to India*, 18.

24. Foucault, *History of Sexuality*, 11.

25. Stam and Spence, "Colonialism, Racism, and Representation," 636.

26. Bhabha, "Articulating the Archaic," 206.

27. Ibid.

28. Ibid.

29. Forster, *A Passage to India*, 230.

30. Said, *Orientalism*, 7.

CHAPTER SIX

1. As cited in Stanley Meisler, "War Turned Impoverished U.S. into a Superpower," *Los Angeles Times*, 31 August 1989, C5.

2. Hurston, *Dust Tracks on a Road*, 341 (hereafter cited in text as *DTR*).

3. Plamenatz, "Two Types of Nationalism," 23–24. Nationalism is neither necessarily good nor evil. It has historically functioned to bring about socially progressive ends as well as much more pernicious ones. However, one could make a case that its manifestations in the twentieth century have, on the whole, brought about more negative than positive social goals.

4. Norris, *The Contest of Faculties*, 83.

5. De Man, *Allegories of Reading*, 80.

6. Lifton and Markusen, *The Genocidal Mentality*, 54.

7. As quoted in ibid., although there this quote is not attributed to Hitler.

8. Van Iersel and Weiler, *Exodus*, xv.

9. Griffin, *God and Religion*, 29. Other qualities that characterize this supernaturalistic model include God's monopoly on power, divine acquiescence in allowing a cosmic power of evil to infect the world, and the belief that in the end time, God will unleash the full destructive capacity of divine omnipotence to rid the world of evil.

10. Ibid., 132.

11. Ibid.

12. Hurston, *Moses, Man of the Mountain* (hereafter cited in text as *MMM*).

13. Gottwald, *The Hebrew Bible*, 137, 140.

14. Kamenka, "Political Nationalism," 4.

15. Culler, *On Deconstruction*, 96.

16. Johnson, *The Critical Difference*, x.

17. Rabine, "A Feminist Politics," 19.

18. Hurston describes the common Christian conception of Moses as follows: "Moses was an old man with a beard. He was the great lawgiver. He had some trouble with Pharaoh about some plagues and led the Children of Israel out of Egypt and on to the Promised Land. He died on Mount Nebo and the angels buried him there" (*Moses, Man of the Mountain*, xxi).

19. Derrida, *Positions*, 42.

20. Rabine, "A Feminist Politics," 18.

21. Anzaldúa, *Borderlands*, 80.

22. Ibid., 79. She draws from the work of José Vasconcelos, the Mexican philosopher who first envisaged *una raza mestiza*.

23. Ibid.

24. Gottwald, *The Hebrew Bible*, 12.

25. Harrison, *Mythology*, 61.

26. Stone, *When God Was a Woman*, 215.

27. See ibid.

28. Gottwald, *The Hebrew Bible*, 199.

29. Eisler, *The Chalice and the Blade*, 193.

30. Ibid., 45.

31. Garvey, *Philosophy and Opinions*, 1:43.

32. Burkett, *Garveyism*, 61.

33. Editorial by Garvey in *Negro World*, as cited in ibid.

34. Christ, *Laughter of Aphrodite*, 75.

35. Ibid., 121.

36. Gadon, *The Once and Future Goddess*, 264.

37. Ibid.

38. Christ, *Laughter of Aphrodite*, 125.

39. Rubin, "The Traffic in Women," 204. There are difficulties with the opposition that Rubin sets up in her theory of the sex/gender system, but it is still an extremely useful construct when combating the biological determinism of certain forms of feminist theory.

40. Flax, *Thinking Fragments*, 149.

41. Koonz, *Mothers in the Fatherland*, 14.

42. As cited in ibid., xix.

43. Ibid., 5.

44. Brown, "Why Women Need the War God," 190–91.

45. Spivak, *Post-Colonial Critic*, 47.

46. Rossi, "Sex Equality," 180.

47. Tong, *Feminist Thought*, 103.

48. Barthes, *Roland Barthes*, 69.

49. Barthes, *The Rustle of Language*, 60.

50. Anzaldúa, *Borderlands*, 80.

51. Terdiman, *Discourse/Counter-Discourse*, 33.

52. Ibid.

53. Norris, *Paul de Man*, 178.

54. Hartmann, "Blindness and Insight," 31, as cited in Norris, *Paul de Man*, 190.

CHAPTER SEVEN

1. Barthelme, "Not-Knowing," 17.

2. Blonsky, "The Agony of Semiotics," xv.

3. Jardine, *Gynesis*, 25.

4. Ibid., 37.

5. Sohn-Rethel, *Intellectual and Manual Labor*, 6.

6. Ibid., 33.

7. De Lauretis, *Alice Doesn't*, 15.

8. Newton and Rosenfelt, Introduction, xx.

9. Goldman, "The Traffic in Women," 20.

10. Schreiner, *From Man to Man*, 72 (hereafter cited in text as *FMM*).

11. Marx, *Capital*, 1:165.

12. Sohn-Rethel, *Intellectual and Manual Labor*, 33.

13. I use the Lacanian term *misprision* advisedly here. For Lacan, misprision occurs during the mirror stage when the infant mistakes its seemingly whole and independent reflection for its own ontological subjectivity. Capitalism forces a similar, yet more sinister, distortion upon its participants, for women's individual and material subjectivity is misrecognized as an abstract and quantitative objectivity.

14. Irigaray, "Women on the Market," 175.

15. Sohn-Rethel, *Intellectual and Manual Labor*, 48–49.

16. Ibid., 25.

17. Hartsock, *Money, Sex, and Power*, 97.

18. This rather whimsical, yet astute, proverb originated with Roland Barthes.

19. Derrida, *Positions*, 81.

20. Derrida, *Spurs*, 221.

21. Derrida, "The Double Session," 221.

22. Felman, "Rereading Femininity," 42.

23. Kristeva, "Woman Can Never Be Defined," 137.

24. Jardine, *Gynesis*, 38.

25. Lévi-Strauss, *Elementary Structures*, 54.

26. Carroll, *The Annotated Alice*, 207–8. At this particular point in the story, Alice, who is a White's pawn, has advanced to Q7, or the square immediately prior to her coronation as Queen. The opposing Red Knight makes a powerful move to attack the White Queen and, in so doing, takes Alice as his prisoner. Immediately, the White Knight claims the square occupied by the Red Knight, and the two do battle. After the White Knight emerges victorious, he remarks, "It was a glorious victory, wasn't it?" "I don't know," Alice says doubtfully. "I don't want to be anybody's prisoner. I want to be a Queen."

27. Lévi-Strauss, *Elementary Structures*, 480.

28. De Lauretis, *Alice Doesn't*, 167.

29. Eco, *A Theory of Semiotics*, 16.

30. Ibid., 26.

31. Lévi-Strauss, *Elementary Structures*, 496.

32. Irigaray, "Women on the Market," 190–91.

33. Schreiner, *Woman and Labor*, 192.

34. Both Hartsock in *Money, Sex, and Power* and Sandra Harding in *The Science Question in Feminism* (Ithaca, N.Y.: Cornell University Press, 1986), 26–68, make this argument.

35. Schreiner, *Woman and Labor*, 27.

36. The fact that this baby is actually the dead twin of Baby Bertie does not change the import of Rebekah's actions. It does, however, suggest that in the present configuration of patriarchal capitalism, such a change of status is almost impossible except in the realm of imagination—which is precisely where Rebekah's self-to-self stories lead us.

37. Schreiner, *Woman and Labor*, 191.

38. Young, "Pregnant Subjectivity," 30.

39. Schreiner, *Woman and Labor*, 191. It is interesting to note that in this passage, Schreiner directly contravenes Simone de Beauvoir's view in *The Second Sex* that the supreme accolade of "human" is given not to the sex that bears life or feels connected with it but to that (masculine) one which kills.

40. Martin and Mohanty, "Feminist Politics," 205.

41. Schreiner, *From Man to Man*, "Note on the Genesis of the Book."

42. De Lauretis, *Alice Doesn't*, 77.

43. Schreiner, *From Man to Man*, "Note on the Genesis of the Book."

44. Clifford, "On Ethnographic Allegory," 100.

45. De Man, "The Rhetoric of Temporality," 207.

46. Kristeva, "From Symbol to Sign," 65.

47. "Horizontal violence" is Flo Kennedy's term for the infighting among members of an oppressed group. Both this term and Wittig's comment are cited in de Lauretis, "Issues, Terms, and Contexts," 7.

48. De Man, "The Rhetoric of Temporality," 209.

49. Jardine, *Gynesis*, 118.

50. Martin and Mohanty, "Feminist Politics," 197. The relation of this view of identity to allegory is my own application of this insight.

51. Clifford, "On Ethnographic Allegory," 103.

POSTSCRIPT

1. Shank, "Freedom and Control," 1.

2. De Lauretis, *Alice Doesn't*, 39.

3. Ibid., 159.

4. O'Brien, *The Politics of Reproduction*, 168.

5. Ibid., 50.

6. King, "Producing Sex, Theory, and Culture," 83.

7. Haraway, *Primate Visions*, 188. Haraway is actually referring to the "origin of man" stories of physical anthropology in this quotation.

Filmography

The King and I (20th Century-Fox, 1956)

CREDITS

Producer	Charles Brackett
Director	Walter Lang
Screenplay	Ernest Lehman
Art Director	Lyle Wheeler and John DeCuir
Musical Director	Alfred Newman
Associate	Ken Darby
Book and Lyrics	Oscar Hammerstein II
Music	Richard Rodgers
Choreography	Jerome Robbins
Costumes	Irene Sharaff

CAST

Mrs. Anna Leonowens	Deborah Kerr (vocals by Marni Nixon)

King Mongkut	Yul Brynner
Tuptim	Rita Moreno
The Kralahome	Martin Benson
Lady Thiang	Terry Saunders
Lun Tha	Carlos Rivas (vocals by Reuben Fuentes)
Louis Leonowens	Rex Thompson
"Eliza"	Yuriko
Simon of Legree	Marion Jim
Uncle Thomas	Dusty Worrall
Angel	Michiki Iseri

A Passage to India (Columbia Pictures, 1984)

CREDITS

Producer	John Brabourne and Richard Goodwin
Director	David Lean
Screenplay	David Lean
Production Supervisor	Barrie Melrose
Production Designer	John Box
Director of Photography	Ernest Day
Editor	David Lean
Assistant Editor	Eunice Mountjoy
Music	Maurice Jarre with the Royal Philharmonic Orchestra
Costume Designer	Judy Moorcroft

CAST

Mrs. Moore	Dame Peggy Ashcroft
Adela Quested	Judy Davis
Ronny Heaslop	Nigel Havers
Cyril Fielding	James Fox
Dr. Aziz	Victor Banerjee
Mr. Turton	Richard Wilson
Mrs. Turton	Antonia Pemberton
McBryde	Michael Culver
Hamidullah	Saeed Jaffrey

Filmography

Mahmoud Ali	Art Malik
Dr. Godbole	Sir Alec Guinness
Major Callendar	Clive Swift
Mrs. Callendar	Ann Firbank
Amritrao	Roshan Seth

We of the Never-Never (Triumph Films, 1983)

CREDITS

Executive Producer	Philip Adams
Producer	Greg Tepper
Coproducer	John B. Murray
Associate Producer	Brian Rosen
Director	Igor Auzins
Screenplay	Peter Schreck
Production Designer	Christine Ford
Director of Photography	Gary Hansen
Editor	Clifford Hayes
Sound Editor	Frank Lipson
Music	Peter Best

CAST

Jeannie Gunn	Angela Punch McGregor
Aeneas Gunn	Arthur Dignam
Dan	Tommy Lewis
Mac	Tony Barry
Jack	Lewis Fitz-Gerald
Goggle Eye	Donald Blitner
Bett-Bett	Sibina Willy
Rosie	Mawuyul Yanthalawuy
Nellie	Jessie Roberts

Bibliography

Ahmed, Leila. "Western Ethnocentrism and Perceptions of the Harem."
  Feminist Studies 8 (1982): 521–34.
Allen, Jeffner. *Lesbian Philosophy: Explorations*. Palo Alto, Calif.:
  Institute of Lesbian Studies, 1986.
Alloula, Malek. *The Colonial Harem*. Introduction by Barbara Har-
  low; translated by Myrna Godzich and Wlad Godzich. Minneapolis:
  University of Minnesota Press, 1986.
Althusser, Louis. *For Marx*. Translated by Ben Brewster. London: Verso
  Press, 1977.
Anzaldúa, Gloria. *Borderlands/La Frontera: The New Mestiza*. San
  Francisco: Spinster/Aunt Lute, 1987.
Ashcroft, Bill, Gareth Griffiths, and Helen Tiffin. *The Empire Strikes
  Back: Theory and Practice in Post-Colonial Literatures*. New York
  and London: Routledge, 1989.
Baker, Houston, Jr. "Caliban's Triple Play." *Critical Inquiry* 13 (1986):
  182–96.
Barrett, Michèle. *Women's Oppression Today: Problems in Marxist
  Feminist Analysis*. 1980. Rev. ed. London: Verso Press, 1988.

Barrie, J. M. *Peter Pan*. Illustrated by Michael Hague. New York: Henry Holt and Company, 1987.

Barthelme, Donald. "Not-Knowing." In *The Best American Essays, 1986*, edited by Elizabeth Hardwick, 9–24. New York: Ticknor and Fields, 1986.

Barthes, Roland. *Roland Barthes*. Translated by Richard Howard. New York: Hill and Wang, 1977.

———. *The Rustle of Language*. Translated by Richard Howard. New York: Hill and Wang, 1986.

———. *The Semiotic Challenge*. Translated by Richard Howard. New York: Hill and Wang, 1988.

Bates, Daisy. *The Passing of the Aborigines: A Lifetime Spent among the Natives of Australia*. Foreword by Alan Moorehead; Introduction by Arthur Mee. 1938. Reprint. New York: Frederick A. Praeger, 1967.

Bearce, George D. *British Attitudes towards India, 1784–1858*. London: Oxford University Press, 1961.

Belsey, Catherine. *Critical Practice*. London: Methuen, 1980.

Bersani, Leo. *A Future for Astyanax: Character and Desire in Literature*. New York: Columbia University Press, 1984.

Bhabha, Homi K. "Articulating the Archaic: Notes on Colonial Nonsense." In *Literary Theory Today*, edited by Peter Collier and Helga Geyer-Ryan, 203–18. Ithaca, N.Y.: Cornell University Press, 1990.

Blonsky, Marshall. "The Agony of Semiotics: Reassessing the Discipline." In *On Signs*, edited by Marshall Blonsky, xiii–li. Baltimore: Johns Hopkins University Press, 1985.

Bourdieu, Pierre. *Outline of a Theory of Practice*. Translated by Richard Nice. New York: Cambridge University Press, 1977.

Bresson, Robert. *Notes on the Cinematographer*. Introduction by J. M. G. LeClezio; translated by Jonathan Griffin. London: Quartet Books, 1975.

Brontë, Charlotte. *Jane Eyre*. Edited by Margaret Smith. London: Oxford University Press, 1973.

Broome, Richard. *Aboriginal Australians: Black Response to White Dominance, 1788–1980*. Sydney: George Allen and Unwin, 1982.

Brown, Karen McCarthy. "Why Women Need the War God." In *Women's Spirit Bonding*, edited by Janet Kalven and Mary I. Buckley, 190–201. New York: Pilgrim Press, 1984.

Bulhan, Hussein Abdilahi. *Frantz Fanon and the Psychology of Oppression*. London: Plenum, 1985.

Burkett, Randall K. *Garveyism as a Religious Movement: The Institutionalization of a Black Civil Religion*. Metuchen, N.J.: Scarecrow

Press and the American Theological Library Association, 1978.

Callinicos, Alex. *Marxism and Philosophy*. New York: Oxford University Press, 1985.

Carroll, Lewis. *The Annotated Alice: Alice's Adventures in Wonderland and Through the Looking Glass*. Introduction and notes by Martin Gardner; illustrated by John Tenniel. New York: New American Library, 1960.

Castoriadis, Cornelius. *The Imaginary Institution of Society*. Translated by Kathleen Blamey. Cambridge: MIT Press, 1987.

Cesaire, Aimé. *Discourse on Colonialism*. Translated by Joan Pinkham. New York: Monthly Review Press, 1972.

Chesler, Phyllis. *Women and Madness*. New York: Doubleday, 1972.

Chodorow, Nancy. *The Reproduction of Mothering: Psychoanalysis and the Sociology of Gender*. Berkeley: University of California Press, 1978.

Christ, Carol P. *Laughter of Aphrodite: Reflections on a Journey to the Goddess*. San Francisco: Harper and Row, 1987.

Clifford, James. "On Ethnographic Allegory." In *Writing Culture: The Poetics and Politics of Ethnography*, edited by James Clifford and George E. Marcus, 98–121. Berkeley and Los Angeles: University of California Press, 1986.

Coward, Rosalind. *Female Desires: How They Are Bought, Sold, and Packaged*. New York: Grove Press, 1985.

Cros, Edmond. *Theory and Practice of Sociocriticism*. Foreword by Jürgen Link and Ursula Link-Heer; translated by Jerome Schwartz. Minneapolis: University of Minnesota Press, 1988.

Culler, Jonathan. *On Deconstruction: Theory and Criticism after Structuralism*. Ithaca, N.Y.: Cornell University Press, 1982.

Davis, Angela. *Women, Race, and Class*. New York: Vintage Books, 1983.

de Certeau, Michel. *Heterologies: Discourse on the Other*. Foreword by Wlad Godzich; translated by Brian Massumi. Minneapolis: University of Minnesota Press, 1986.

de Lauretis, Teresa. *Alice Doesn't: Feminism, Semiotics, Cinema*. Bloomington: Indiana University Press, 1984.

———. "Issues, Terms, and Contexts." In *Feminist Studies, Critical Studies*, edited by Teresa de Lauretis, 1–19. Bloomington: Indiana University Press, 1986.

———. *Technologies of Gender: Essays on Theory, Film, and Fiction*. Bloomington: Indiana University Press, 1987.

de Man, Paul. *Allegories of Reading: Figural Language in Rousseau*,

Nietzsche, Rilke, and Proust. New Haven: Yale University Press, 1979.

———. "The Rhetoric of Temporality." In *Blindness and Insight: The Rhetoric of Contemporary Criticism*, 2d ed., Introduction by Wlad Godzich, 187–228. Minneapolis: University of Minnesota Press, 1983.

Derrida, Jacques. "The Double Session." In *Dissemination*, translated by Barbara Johnson, 173–286. Chicago: University of Chicago Press, 1981.

———. *Positions.* Translated by Alan Bass. Chicago: University of Chicago Press, 1981.

———. *Spurs: Nietzsche's Styles.* Introduction by Stefano Agosti; translated by Barbara Harlow. Chicago: University of Chicago Press, 1981.

Donovan, Josephine. "Afterword: Critical Re-vision." In *Feminist Literary Criticism: Explorations in Theory*, edited by Josephine Donovan, 74–82. Lexington: University of Kentucky Press, 1975.

———. "Towards a Women's Poetics." In *Feminist Issues in Literary Scholarship*, edited by Shari Benstock, 98–109. Bloomington: University of Indiana Press, 1987.

Douglass, Frederick. *The Life and Writings of Frederick Douglass.* 3 vols. Edited by Philip S. Foner. New York: International Publishers, 1950.

Doyle, Michael W. *Empires.* Ithaca, N.Y.: Cornell University Press, 1986.

Dunbar, Janet. *J. M. Barrie: The Man behind the Image.* Boston: Houghton Mifflin, 1970.

Eagleton, Terry. *Ideology: An Introduction.* New York: Verso Press, 1991.

———. *Literary Theory: An Introduction.* Minneapolis: University of Minnesota Press, 1983.

Eco, Umberto. *The Role of the Reader: An Exploration in the Semiotics of Texts.* Bloomington: Indiana University Press, 1979.

———. *A Theory of Semiotics.* Bloomington: Indiana University Press, 1976.

Eisenstein, Zillah. "Developing a Theory of Capitalist Patriarchy and Socialist Feminism." In *Capitalist Patriarchy and the Case for Socialist Feminism*, edited by Zillah Eisenstein, 5–40. New York: Monthly Review Press, 1979.

Eisler, Riane. *The Chalice and the Blade: Our History, Our Future.* San Francisco: Harper and Row, 1987.

Ellison, Ralph. *Invisible Man*. New York: Vintage Books, 1952.

Ethnic Notions. Documentary video created, produced, and directed by Marlon Riggs. San Francisco: KQED, 1987.

Etienne, Mona, and Eleanor Leacock, eds. *Women and Colonization: Anthropological Perspectives*. New York: Praeger, 1980.

Fanon, Frantz. *Black Skin, White Masks*. Translated by Charles Lam Markmann. New York: Grove Press, 1967.

Felman, Shosanna. "Rereading Femininity." *Yale French Studies* 62 (1981): 19–44.

Feral, Josette. "The Powers of Difference." In *The Future of Difference*, edited by Hester Eisenstein and Alice Jardine, 88–94. Boston: G. K. Hall and Company, Barnard College Women's Center, 1980.

Feuer, Jane. *The Hollywood Musical*. Bloomington: Indiana University Press, 1982.

Flax, Jane. *Thinking Fragments: Psychoanalysis, Feminism, and Postmodernism in the Contemporary West*. Berkeley and Los Angeles: University of California Press, 1990.

Forster, E. M. *A Passage to India*. New York: Harcourt Brace Jovanovich, 1924.

Foucault, Michel. "Discourse on Language." In *The Archaeology of Knowledge*, translated by A. M. Sheridan Smith, 215–37. New York: Harper and Row, 1972.

———. *The History of Sexuality*. Vol. 1, *An Introduction*, translated by Robert Hurley. New York: Vintage Books, 1980.

Fowler, Roger. *Literature as Social Discourse: The Practice of Linguistic Criticism*. Bloomington: Indiana University Press, 1981.

Freire, Paulo. *Pedagogy of the Oppressed*. Translated by Myra Bergman Ramos. New York: Continuum Publishing, 1970.

French, Marilyn. *Beyond Power: On Men, Women, and Morals*. New York: Ballantine Books, 1985.

———. *The Women's Room*. New York: Jove Publications, 1977.

Freud, Sigmund. "On Narcissism: An Introduction." In *General Psychological Theory: Papers on Metapsychology*, Introduction by Philip Rieff, 56–82. New York: Collier Books, 1963.

Frye, Marilyn. "Some Reflections on Separatism and Power." In *The Politics of Reality: Essays in Feminist Theory*. Trumansburg, N.Y.: The Crossing Press, 1983.

Gadon, Elinor W. *The Once and Future Goddess: A Symbol for Our Time*. San Francisco: Harper and Row, 1989.

Galeano, Eduardo. *Memory of Fire*. Vol. 2, *Faces and Masks*, translated by Cedric Befrage. New York: Pantheon Books, 1987.

Garner, R. J. *The Grafter's Handbook.* New York: Oxford University Press, 1979.

Garvey, Marcus. *Philosophy and Opinions.* Edited by Amy Jacques-Garvey; Introduction by Hollis R. Lynch. 2 vols. New York: Atheneum, 1974.

Gates, Henry Louis, Jr. "The Blackness of Blackness: A Critique of the Sign and the Signifying Monkey." In *Black Literature and Literary Theory,* edited by Henry Louis Gates, Jr., 285–321. New York: Methuen, 1984.

———. "Writing 'Race' and the Difference It Makes." *Critical Inquiry* 12 (1985): 1–20.

Gilbert, Sandra M., and Susan Gubar. *The Madwoman in the Attic: The Woman Writer and the Nineteenth-Century Imagination.* New Haven: Yale University Press, 1984.

Goldman, Emma. "The Traffic in Women." In *The Traffic in Women and Other Essays on Feminism,* 19–32. Washington, N.J.: Times Change Press, 1970.

Goontilake, Susantha. *Crippled Minds: An Exploration into Colonial Culture.* New Delhi: Vikas Publishing House, 1982.

Gottwald, Norman. *The Hebrew Bible: A Socio-Literary Introduction.* Philadelphia: Fortress Press, 1985.

Gramsci, Antonio. *Selections from the Cultural Writings.* Edited by David Forgacs and Geoffrey Nowell-Smith; translated by William Boelhower. Boston: Harvard University Press, 1985.

Griffin, David Ray. *God and Religion in the Postmodern World: Essays in Postmodern Theology.* Albany: State University of New York Press, 1989.

Gunn, Mrs. Aeneas. *The Little Black Princess.* 1905. Reprint. New York: Avon Books, 1982.

———. *We of the Never-Never.* 1905. Reprint. New York: Avon Books, 1982.

Habermas, Jürgen. *Knowledge and Human Interests.* Translated by Jeremy J. Shapiro. Boston: Beacon Press, 1971.

———. *The Philosophical Discourse of Modernity: Twelve Lectures.* Translated by Frederick Lawrence. Cambridge: MIT Press, 1987.

Haraway, Donna. *Primate Visions: Gender, Race, and Nature in the World of Modern Science.* New York: Routledge, 1988.

Harrison, Jane Ellen. *Mythology.* Boston: Marshall Jones Company, 1924.

Hartmann, Geoffrey. "Blindness and Insight." *New Republic*, 7 March 1988, 31.

Hartsock, Nancy. *Money, Sex, and Power: Toward a Feminist Historical Materialism*. Boston: Northeastern University Press, 1985.

Heath, Stephen. *Questions of Cinema*. Bloomington: Indiana University Press, 1981.

Held, David. *Introduction to Critical Theory: Horkheimer to Habermas*. Berkeley and Los Angeles: University of California Press, 1980.

Holly, Marcia. "Consciousness and Authenticity: Toward a Feminist Aesthetic." In *Feminist Literary Criticism: Explorations in Theory*, edited by Josephine Donovan, 38–47. Lexington: University of Kentucky Press, 1975.

hooks, bell [Gloria Watkins]. *Ain't I a Woman?: Black Women and Feminism*. Boston: South End Press, 1981.

———. *Yearning: Race, Gender, and Cultural Politics*. Boston: South End Press, 1990.

Hurston, Zora Neale. *Dust Tracks on a Road: An Autobiography*. 2d ed., edited by Robert Hemenway. Urbana: University of Illinois Press, 1984.

———. *Moses, Man of the Mountain*. Introduction by Blyden Jackson. Urbana: University of Illinois Press, 1939.

———. *Mules and Men*. Preface by Franz Boaz; Introduction by Robert Hemenway. Bloomington: Indiana University Press, 1963.

Irigaray, Luce. "Women on the Market." In *This Sex Which Is Not One*, translated by Catherine Porter with Carolyn Burke, 170–91. Ithaca, N.Y.: Cornell University Press, 1985.

Jardine, Alice. *Gynesis: Configurations of Woman and Modernity*. Ithaca, N.Y.: Cornell University Press, 1985.

Jayawardena, Kumari. *Feminism and Nationalism in the Third World*. London: Zed Books, 1986.

Johnson, Barbara. *The Critical Difference: Essays in the Contemporary Rhetoric of Reading*. Baltimore: Johns Hopkins University Press, 1980.

Johnston, Claire. "Towards a Feminist Film Practice: Some Theses." In *Movies and Methods*, vol. 2, edited by Bill Nichols, 315–27. Berkeley and Los Angeles: University of California Press, 1985.

Kamenka, Eugene. "Political Nationalism: The Evolution of the Idea." In *Nationalism: The Nature and Evolution of an Idea*, edited by Eugene Kamenka. London: Edward Arnold, 1976.

Kaplan, E. Ann. *Women and Film: Both Sides of the Camera*. London: Methuen, 1983.

King, Katie. "Producing Sex, Theory, and Culture: Gay/Straight Remappings in Contemporary Feminism." In *Conflicts in Feminism*, edited by Marianne Hirsch and Evelyn Fox Keller, 82–104. New York: Routledge, 1990.

Koonz, Claudia. *Mothers in the Fatherland: Women, the Family, and Nazi Politics*. New York: St. Martin's Press, 1987.

Kristeva, Julia. "From Symbol to Sign." In *The Kristeva Reader*, edited by Toril Moi, 62–73. New York: Columbia University Press, 1986.

——— . *Language, the Unknown: An Initiation into Linguistics*. Translated by Anne M. Menke. New York: Columbia University Press, 1989.

——— . "Woman Can Never Be Defined." In *New French Feminisms: An Anthology*, edited by Elaine Marks and Isabelle de Courtivron, 137–41. New York: Schocken Books, 1981.

Kuhn, Annette. *Women's Pictures: Feminism and Cinema*. London: Routledge and Kegan Paul, 1982.

Laclau, Ernesto, and Chantal Mouffe. *Hegemony and Socialist Strategy: Towards a Radical Democratic Politics*. Translated by Winston Moore and Paul Cammack. London: Verso Press, 1985.

Landon, Margaret. *Anna and the King of Siam*. New York: John Day Company, 1944.

Lehman, Ernest. "The King and I." Revised final screenplay, 4 October 1955.

Leonowens, Anna Harriette. *The English Governess at the Siamese Court: Being Recollections of Six Years in the Royal Palace at Bangkok*. Boston: Fields, Osgood, and Company, 1870.

——— . *Siamese Harem Life*. Introduction by Freya Stark. 1873. Reprint. New York: Dutton, 1953.

Lévi-Strauss, Claude. *The Elementary Structures of Kinship*. Rev. ed., translated by James Harle Bell, John Richard von Sturmer, and Rodney Needham. Boston: Beacon Press, 1969.

Lifton, Robert Jay, and Eric Markusen. *The Genocidal Mentality: Nazi Holocaust and Nuclear Threat*. New York: Basic Books, 1990.

Link, Jürgen, and Ursula Link-Heer. Foreword to *Theory and Practice of Sociocriticism*, by Edmond Cros; translated by Jerome Schwartz, vi–xviii. Minneapolis: University of Minnesota Press, 1988.

MacCabe, Colin. "On Discourse." In *Tracking the Signifier: Theoretical Essays—Film, Linguistics, Literature*, 82–112. Minneapolis: University of Minnesota Press, 1985.

McDowell, Deborah E. "New Directions for Black Feminist Criticism." In *The New Feminist Criticism: Essays on Women, Literature, and*

Theory, edited by Elaine Showalter, 186–99. New York: Pantheon Books, 1985.

Martin, Biddy, and Chandra Talpade Mohanty. "Feminist Politics: What's Home Got to Do with It?" In *Feminist Studies, Critical Studies*, edited by Teresa de Lauretis, 191–212. Bloomington: Indiana University Press, 1986.

Marx, Karl. *Capital: A Critique of Political Economy*. Introduction by Ernest Mandel; translated by Ben Fowkes. 3 vols. 1867. Reprint. New York: Vintage Books, 1977.

Meese, Elizabeth A. *(Ex)tensions: Re-figuring Feminist Criticism*. Urbana: University of Illinois Press, 1990.

Memmi, Albert. *The Colonizer and the Colonized*. Introduction by Jean-Paul Sartre. Boston: Beacon Press, 1965.

Millett, Kate. *Sexual Politics*. Garden City, N.Y.: Doubleday, 1970.

Mitchell, Juliet. *Women: The Longest Revolution*. New York: Pantheon Books, 1984.

Mohanty, Chandra Talpade. "Under Western Eyes: Feminist Scholarship and Colonial Discourses." In *Third World Women and the Politics of Feminism*, edited by Chandra Talpade Mohanty, Ann Russo, and Lourdes Torres, 51–80. Bloomington: Indiana University Press, 1991.

Monaco, James. *How to Read a Film: The Art, Technology, Language, History, and Theory of Film and Media*. Rev. ed. Oxford: Oxford University Press, 1981.

Moorehead, Alan. Foreword to *The Passing of the Aborigines: A Lifetime Spent among the Natives of Australia*, by Daisy Bates. 1938. Reprint. New York: Frederick A. Praeger, 1967.

Mulvey, Laura. "Visual Pleasure and Narrative Cinema." In *Film Theory and Criticism: Introductory Readings*, 3d ed., edited by Gerald Mast and Marshall Cohen, 803–16. Oxford: Oxford University Press, 1985.

Newton, Judith, and Deborah Rosenfelt. Introduction to *Feminist Criticism and Social Change: Sex, Class, and Race in Literature and Culture*, xv–xxxix. New York: Methuen, 1985.

Norris, Christopher. *The Contest of Faculties: Philosophy and Theory after Deconstruction*. New York: Methuen, 1985.

————. *Paul de Man: Deconstruction and the Critique of Aesthetic Ideology*. New York: Routledge and Kegan Paul, 1988.

Nyerere, Julius K. *Freedom and Socialism/Uhuru na Ujamaa: A Selection from Writings and Speeches, 1965–1967*. Dar es Salaam, Tanzania: Oxford University Press, 1968.

O'Brien, Mary. *The Politics of Reproduction*. Boston: Routledge and Kegan Paul, 1981.

Ogunyemi, Chikwenye Okonjo. "Womanism: The Dynamics of the Contemporary Black Female Novel in English." *Signs: Journal of Women in Culture and Society* 11 (1985): 63–80.

Pasolini, Pier Paolo. *Heretical Empiricism*. Edited by Louise K. Barnett; translated by Ben Lawton and Louise K. Barnett. Bloomington: Indiana University Press, 1988.

Plamenatz, John. "Two Types of Nationalism." In *Nationalism: The Nature and Evolution of an Idea*, edited by Eugene Kamenka, 22–36. London: Edward Arnold, 1976.

Price, Susan. "Images of Empire." *Los Angeles Times Magazine*, 30 August 1987, 32.

Przybylowicz, Donna. "Toward a Feminist Cultural Criticism: Hegemony and Modes of Social Division." *Cultural Critique* 14 (1989–90): 259–301.

Pudovkin, Vsevolod. "On Editing." In *Film Theory and Criticism: Introductory Readings*, 3d ed., edited by Gerald Mast and Marshall Cohen, 83–89. Oxford: Oxford University Press, 1985.

Rabine, Leslie Wahl. "A Feminist Politics of Non-identity." *Feminist Studies* 14 (1988): 11–31.

Reader's Digest Illustrated Guide to Gardening. Edited by Carroll C. Calkins. Pleasantville, N.Y.: Reader's Digest, 1978.

Register, Cheri. "American Feminist Literary Criticism: A Bibliographical Introduction." In *Feminist Literary Criticism: Explorations in Theory*, edited by Josephine Donovan, 1–28. Lexington: University of Kentucky Press, 1975.

Rich, Adrienne. "Disloyal to Civilization: Feminism, Racism, Gynephobia." In *On Lies, Secrets, and Silence: Selected Prose, 1966–1978*, 275–310. New York: W. W. Norton and Company, 1979.

Ricoeur, Paul. "The Hermeneutical Function of Distanciation." In *Hermeneutics and the Human Sciences: Essays on Language, Action, and Interpretation*, edited and translated by John B. Thompson, 131–44. London: Cambridge University Press; Paris: Edition de la Maison des Sciences de l'Homme, 1981.

Rossi, Alice. "Sex Equality: The Beginning of Ideology." In *Masculine/Feminine: Readings in Sexual Mythology and the Liberation of Women*, edited by Betty Roszak and Theodore Roszak, 173–85. New York: Harper and Row, 1969.

Rowbotham, Sheila. *Women, Resistance, and Revolution: A History of*

Women and Revolution in the Modern World. New York: Vintage Books, 1972.

Rubin, Gayle. "The Traffic in Women: Notes on the Political Economy of Sex." In *Toward an Anthropology of Women,* edited by Rayna R. Reiter, 157–210. New York: Monthly Review Press, 1975.

Said, Edward. *Orientalism.* New York: Vintage Books, 1978.

———. "Through Gringo Eyes: With Conrad in Latin America." *Harper's Magazine,* April 1988, 70–72.

Salusinszky, Imre, ed. *Criticism in Society.* New York: Methuen, 1987.

Schreiner, Olive. *From Man to Man.* Introduction by S. C. Cronwright-Schreiner. Chicago: Academy Press, 1977.

———. *Woman and Labor.* Preface by Jane Graves. 1978. Reprint. London: Virago, 1985.

Sedgwick, Eve Kosofsky. *Between Men: English Literature and Male Homosocial Desire.* New York: Columbia University Press, 1985.

Shank, Gary. "Freedom and Control in Semiotic Inquiry." *Semiotic Scene* 2 (1990): 1–2.

Shepard, Richard F. "The Once—and Still—King Yul." *New York Times,* 27 April 1977.

Showalter, Elaine. "Critical Cross-Dressing: Male Feminists and the Woman of the Year." In *Men in Feminism,* edited by Alice Jardine and Paul Smith, 116–32. New York: Methuen, 1987.

———. "Feminist Criticism in the Wilderness" and "Toward a Feminist Poetics." In *The New Feminist Criticism: Essays on Women, Literature, and Theory,* edited by Elaine Showalter, 125–43, 243–70. New York: Pantheon Books, 1985.

Silverman, David, and Brian Torode. *The Material Word: Some Theories of Language and Its Limits.* London: Routledge and Kegan Paul, 1980.

Silverman, Kaja. *The Acoustic Mirror: The Female Voice in Psychoanalysis and Cinema.* Bloomington: Indiana University Press, 1988.

———. "Histoire d'O: The Construction of a Female Subject." In *Pleasure and Danger: Exploring Female Sexuality,* edited by Carole S. Vance, 320–49. Boston: Routledge and Kegan Paul, 1984.

———. *The Subject of Semiotics.* Oxford: Oxford University Press, 1983.

Smith, Barbara. Introduction to *Home Girls: A Black Feminist Anthology,* edited by Barbara Smith, xix–lvi. New York: Kitchen Table, Women of Color Press, 1983.

———. "Toward a Black Feminist Criticism." In *The New Feminist*

Criticism: Essays on Women, Literature, and Theory, edited by
Elaine Showalter, 168–85. New York: Pantheon Books, 1985.

Sohn-Rethel, Alfred. *Intellectual and Manual Labor: A Critique of
Epistemology*. Translated by Martin Sohn-Rethel. Atlantic Highlands,
N.J.: Humanities Press, 1978.

Spivak, Gayatri Chakravorty. *In Other Worlds: Essays in Cultural
Politics*. New York: Methuen, 1987.

———. *The Post-Colonial Critic: Interviews, Strategies, Dialogues*.
Edited by Sarah Harasym. New York: Routledge, Chapman, and
Hall, 1990.

———. "Three Women's Texts and a Critique of Imperialism." *Critical
Inquiry* 12 (1985): 243–61.

Stam, Robert, and Louise Spence. "Colonialism, Racism, and Representation: An Introduction." In *Movies and Methods*, 2 vols., edited
by Bill Nichols, 2:632–48. Berkeley and Los Angeles: University of
California Press, 1985.

Stone, Merlin. *When God Was a Woman*. New York: Harcourt Brace
Jovanovich, 1976.

Stowe, Harriet Beecher. *Uncle Tom's Cabin, or Life Among the Lowly*.
Edited by Ann Douglas. Hammondsworth, Eng.: Penguin Books,
1981.

Teish, Luisah. *Jambalaya: The Natural Woman's Book of Personal
Charms and Practical Rituals*. San Francisco: Harper and Row, 1985.

———. "Women's Spirituality: A Household Act." In *Home Girls: A
Black Feminist Anthology*, edited by Barbara Smith, 331–51. New
York: Kitchen Table, Women of Color Press, 1983.

Terdiman, Richard. *Discourse/Counter-Discourse: The Theory and
Practice of Symbolic Resistance in Nineteenth-Century France*.
Ithaca, N.Y.: Cornell University Press, 1985.

Todd, Janet. *Feminist Literary History*. New York: Routledge, 1988.

Tompkins, Jane P. *Reader-Response Criticism: From Formalism to
Post-Structuralism*. Baltimore: Johns Hopkins University Press, 1980.

———. "Sentimental Power: *Uncle Tom's Cabin* and the Politics of Lit-
erary History." In *The New Feminist Criticism: Essays on Women,
Literature, and Theory*, edited by Elaine Showalter, 81–104. New
York: Pantheon Books, 1985.

Tong, Rosemarie. *Feminist Thought: A Comprehensive Introduction*.
Boulder, Colo.: Westview Press, 1989.

Van Iersel, Bas, and Anton Weiler, eds. *Exodus—A Lasting Paradigm*.
Eng. lang. ed. Marcus Lefebure. Edinburgh: T. and T. Clark, 1987.

Weedon, Chris. *Feminist Practice and Poststructuralist Theory*. Oxford: Basil Blackwell, 1987.

Woolf, Virginia. *A Room of One's Own*. New York: Harcourt Brace Jovanovich, 1929.

————. *Three Guineas*. New York: Harcourt Brace Jovanovich, 1938.

Young, Iris. "Pregnant Subjectivity and the Limits of Existential Phenomenology." In *Descriptions*, edited by Don Ihde and Hugh J. Silverman, 25–34. Albany: State University of New York Press, 1985.

Index

of death, 30; patriarchal, 37–38, 95; trickle-down, 44; and signifying practices, 60, 89

Colonizer/colonized: as feminist metaphor, 5–7, 28; as false dichotomy, 66–67

Contextualism: and images of women, 35, 54; and African American literature, 55

Deconstruction, 3; and the politics of identity, 10, 117

De Man, Paul, 104, 117

Derrida, Jacques, 108, 117, 125; "The Double Session," 56

Desire, 89; and "India," 90–93, 95, 97, 98; as metonymy, 94–95, 101; overdetermination of, 97

Différance: and deconstruction, 108, 117; as *mestiza* consciousness, 109, 115; and identity, 117

Difference: within women, 2, 34; sexual, 11, 33, 58, 95, 116; and Aryanism, 104

Discourse: and colonialism, 4, 7, 70–72, 85; power-knowledge within, 43, 85; and colonial Catholicism, 71; and distorted communication, 84; fellowships of, 84–85

Empire: and political control, 69; definition of, 79; as commodity, 89

Enthymeme, 72; and the "piccaninny," 76, 84; and abortion, 76–77; as articulatory practice, 78; of Mrs. Gunn, 84

Eshu, 19

Ethnography: and allegory, 134

Exchange: as game, 126–27; of women, 127

Exchange abstraction: and commodity fetishism, 120, 122; as patriarchal construct, 121, 123; and postmodernism, 126

Exodus: and *Uncle Tom's Cabin*, 45–46, 48; and ethnocentrism, 105; as anticolonialist paradigm, 105, 106

Exoticism: and "India," 90; and cinematic spectacle, 92

Experience: as contested site, 136–39; as semiotic category, 137

Feminism: and nationalism, 9; metaphysical-discursive, 34

Fetishism: commodity, 18, 122; of women in film, 26; in *Jane Eyre*, 26–28; of Anna Leonowens, 38–39

Film score: as ideological glue, 100

Freud, Sigmund, 18, 86

Garvey, Marcus, 112

Gaze: and colonialism, 7, 20, 95–96; Phallic, 26–27; and Anna Leonowens, 38–39; Western, 100

Gender: contradictory character of, 2, 116

Goddess: Hathor, 110; as Cosmic Egg, 111; and the warrior God, 112; ethnocentrism of, 113

Goldman, Emma, 122

Graf(ph)ting: textual, 56; feminist trope, 57, 61; and reader-response criticism, 59, 61; as political corruption, 59–60, 62, 65; negative, 62

Grafting: etymology of, 56, 59; horticultural, 56, 59

Gynocriticism, 54, 57; and sexual difference, 33

Harems: and angelic motherhood, 42; discourses of, 43

Hartman, Geoffrey, 117

Hermeneutics of suspicion, 11, 18–19

Heterosexism, 2

Homosocial: relations of imperialism, 8

Hoodoo: as reading strategy, 20

Hurston, Zora Neale: "Seeing the World as It Is," 103, 104, 113; against imperialism, 103, 106

Ideal speech situation: in *We of the Never-Never*, 80, 83; and distorted communication, 82, 84

Ideology: definition, 60; and the reader/viewer, 61

Images of women: contextual approach of, 35, 54–55

Imperialism: and World War II, 106

Interpellation: and the realist text, 21; and gender, 22–23; and suture, 23, 27

Intertextuality: of *The King and I*, 34, 45; and *Uncle Tom's Cabin*, 39–42

Invisible Man, 13–14

Jane Eyre: as feminist limit text, 15; filmic qualities of, 22; as parody, 22; fetishism in, 26–28;

and individualist subjectivity, 27

Knowledge: and power, 70–71, 84–85

Lugones, Maria, 137

Luxemburg, Rosa, 9

Marx, Karl, 71, 130, 138; and hermeneutics of suspicion, 18; *Das Kapital*, 72

Marxism, 3, 7, 11, 87; classical, 6; and discourse, 71, 75, 78; base/superstructure model of, 72, 78, 85. *See also* Colonialism; Discourse

Mason, Bertha, 139; as woman from colonies, 3; as madwoman in the attic, 14; as self-consolidating other, 15; and suicide, 29–30

Meisel, Perry, 118

Mestiza: consciousness, 109, 115; and différance, 115–16

Metonymy: and colonial moment, 6; and desire, 93–101; processes of displacement in, 95, 97–98

Miranda Complex, 1, 139; and hermeneutics of seeing, 16; and contradiction, 17

Misprision: of Miranda Complex, 1; capitalist, 123

Montage: and geo-political awareness, 91; Eisensteinian, 91, 94; parallel, 93, 95–97

Moore, Thomas, 92–93

Moses: in *The King and I*, 45–46; and différance, 108, 116

Motherhood: reproduction of,

22; angelic, 35, 41, 48; moral, 40–41; and Nazism, 114; Schreiner's allegorical vision of, 130–31

Nation: concept of, 8
Nationalism: African, 9; and "Third World" feminism, 9; and race pride, 9, 103; critiques of, 10, 103; and Woolf, 10–11; and Hurston, 10–11, 104; and organicism, 103–4, 117
National Women's Studies Association, 136
Nyerere, Julius, 9

O'Neale, Sondra, 136
Organicism: literary, 103; and Nazi biomedical vision, 104; and nationalism, 104, 108. *See also* Nationalism
Orientalism, 101; and fantasy, 93; and sexuality, 98

Palimpsest: as woman's text, 18–19, 31
Pan-Africanism, 112
Piccaninny: as racist discourse, 7, 75–76, 84, 86; and Tiger Lily, 75; and sexism, 77–78, 86; as distorted communication, 83
Pluralism: conservatism of, 115; and différance, 115; radical, 115; bourgeois-libertarian, 115, 116; and androgyny, 116
Pomba Gira, 19
Postcolonialism: and subjectivity, 8
Postfeminism, 1
Poststructuralism, 4; and critique

of identity, 11; and Diacritical covergirl, 53
Practice: articulatory, 72, 78–79, 86; and cultural production, 89; semiotic, 133
Prospero Complex, 16–17
Pyramid: as hierarchical construct, 111

Quattrocentric codes, 91, 96

Raj, British, 88, 101
Rape: and Caliban, 17; attempted, 96, 99; individualist psychology of, 100–101; in *From Man to Man*, 121–22
Reproduction: as dialectical process, 138
Ringgold, Faith, 113
Romance: ideology of, 48, 57; in *A Passage to India*, 90

Sati, 50; and the politics of reading, 29–30
Scholtz-Klink, Gertrud: and motherhood, 114; *The Woman in the Third Reich*, 114
Schreiner, Olive: *Woman and Labor*, 121; allegorical vision of motherhood, 129–33
Semiosis: of patriarchal culture, 127
Semiotics: materialist-feminist, 120–21, 128–29, 135, 138
Sentimental novel: and *Uncle Tom's Cabin*, 40. See also *Uncle Tom's Cabin*
Slavery, 15, 35, 105; escape patterns of, 41
Sociocriticism, 64